ON JACK SMITH'S

Flaming Creatures

(AND OTHER SECRET-FLIX OF CINEMAROC)

Marion and Fra
lipstick.

ON JACK SMITH'S

Flaming Creatures

(AND OTHER SECRET-FLIX OF CINEMAROC)

BY J. HOBERMAN

GRANARY BOOKS/HIPS ROAD NYC

TEXT BY
J. Hoberman
©2001

PHOTOGRAPHS BY
Norman Solomon
©2001 Norman Solomon and The Plaster Foundation

PHOTOGRAPHS AND FILM STILLS BY
Ken Jacobs
©2001 Ken Jacobs

ALL OTHER PHOTOGRAPHS, FILM STILLS, AND GRAPHIC MATERIAL
©2001 The Plaster Foundation

FIRST PUBLISHED IN 2001 BY
Granary Books and Hips Road

A PROJECT OF
Hips Road

PRINTED AND BOUND IN
The United States of America

Library of Congress cataloging-publication data
Hoberman, J.
    On Jack Smith's Flaming creatures (and other secret-flix of cinemaroc) / by J. Hoberm
        p.cm.
    ISBN 1-887123-52-0 (pbk. : alk. paper)
    1. Flaming creatures (Motion picture) 2. Experimental films—History and criticism. I.
    Title.

    PN1997.F54 H63 2001
    791.43'72—dc21   20010403

DISTRIBUTED TO THE TRADE BY   GRANARY BOOKS, INC.
D.A.P./Distributed Art Publishers   307 Seventh Avenue, Suite 14
155 Avenue of the Americas   New York, NY 10001
Second Floor   www.granarybooks.com
New York, NY 10013-1507   orders@granarybooks.com
TEL: (212) 627-1999
FAX: (212) 627-9484
ORDERS: (800) 338-BOOK

CONTENTS

On Flaming Creatures

Flaming Creatures frame enlargement (TONY CONRAD, left)

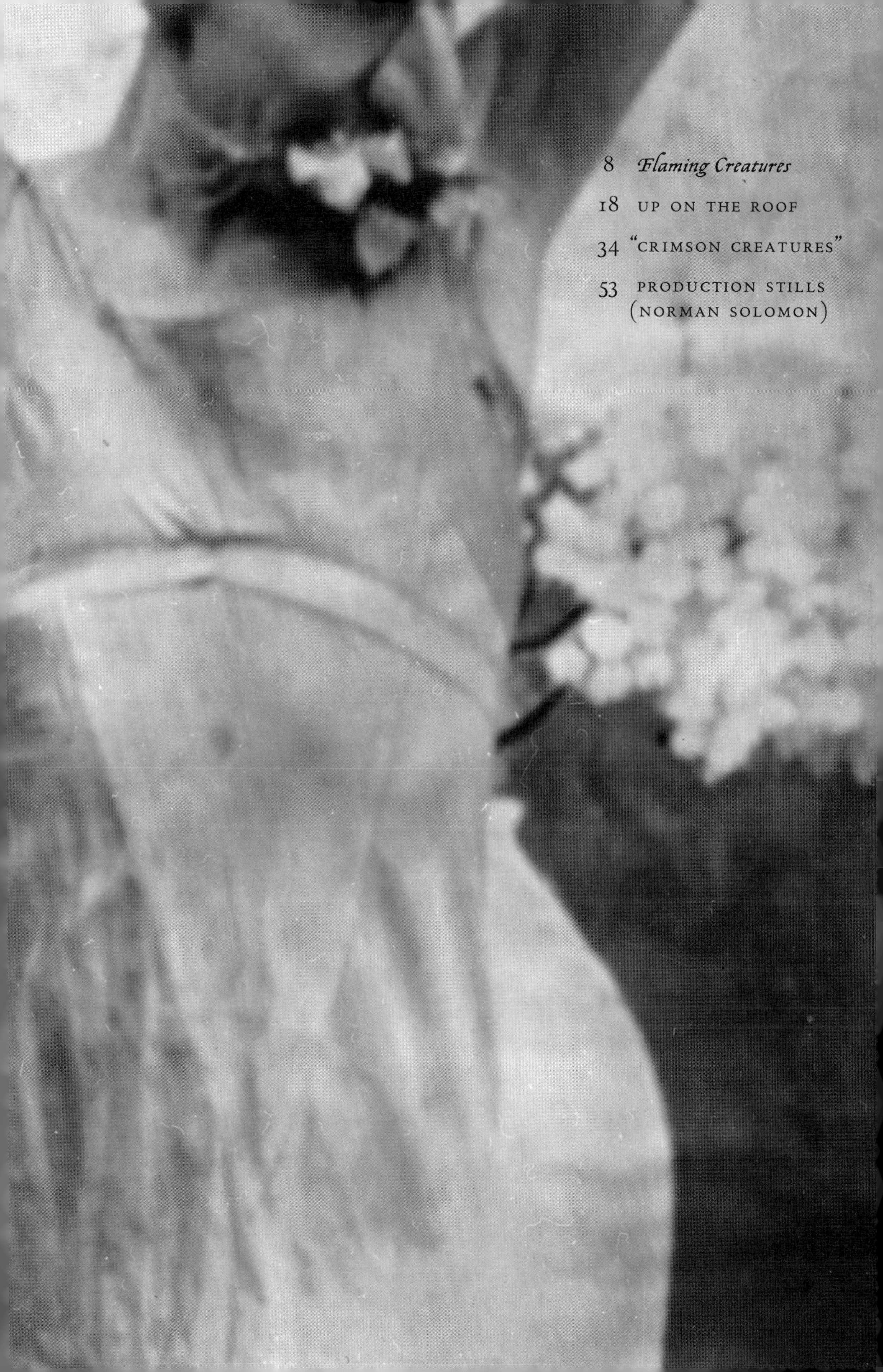

Flaming

[1] Dolores Flores, born Rene Rivera, is better known as Mario Montez. Arnold is Arnold Rockwood. According to Marian Zazeela, who created the credits, Malina declined Smith's offer to reconfigure her name as "Judith Medina."

Flaming Creature's numerous uncredited participants include Tony Conrad; David Gurin; Kate Heliczer; Piero Heliczer; Ray Johnson; Angus MacLise; Ed Marshall; Henry Proach; Jerry Raphael; Irving Rosenthal; Mark Schleifer; Harvey Tavel; Ronald Tavel; John Weiners; LaMonte Young; the granddaughter of the owner of the neighborhood kosher Chinese restaurant, Bernstein-on-Essex; and a bemused-looking sailor who—according to Zazeela—Smith had "plucked off the street."

Assistant director Schleifer, Marian Zazeela's amicably estranged husband, had as his major role (per one participant) "roaming around town trying to get a coffin." As a recent contributor to *Film Culture*, Schleifer also helped Smith get his essay "The Perfect Filmic Appositeness of Maria Montez" in shape for publication.

MARIO MONTEZ

Creatures

Flaming Creatures frame
sequence (SHEILA BICK)

[2] Tony Conrad has released
two excerpts from the
Flaming Creatures
soundtrack on CD. *Jack
Smith: Les Evening
Gowns Damnées* (TABLE
OF THE ELEMENTS, 1997)
includes nearly four
minutes of Earthquake
Orgy: "Screams by Jack
Smith, Mario Montez,
Arnold Rockwood, and
Kate and Piero Heliczer."
Conrad dates the material
to early 1962 (most likely
a misprint for early 1963)
and notes that this "tape
delay loop technique
was introduced in Tony
Conrad's composition
Three Loops, first performed
on December 18, 1961."
*Jack Smith: Silent Shadows
on Cinemaroc Island*
(TABLE OF THE ELEMENTS,
1997) includes three
minutes and 20 seconds
of the Carnival of Ecstasy
mix, recorded 1963,
but does not specify
the components.

JACK SMITH, 1962–63, 42 MINS. B&W.

CAST: Francis Francine (HIMSELF), Delicious Dolores (SHEILA BICK), Our
Lady of the Docks (JOEL MARKMAN), The Spanish Girl (DOLORES FLORES),
Arnold (ARNOLD), The Fascinating Woman (JUDITH MALINA), and Maria
Zazeela (MARIAN ZAZEELA).

PHOTOGRAPHY: Jack Smith. ASSISTANT DIRECTOR: Marc Schleifer.
RECORDING: Tony Conrad. SPECIAL ASSISTANT: Dick Preston.
FACILITIES: The Windsor Theater [1]

MUSIC (UNCREDITED): *Amapola* (VOCAL: DEANNA DURBIN) from
First Love (UNIVERSAL, 1939), *China Nights* (VOCAL: YOSHIKO YAMIGUCHI)
from *China Night* (TOHO, 1940), *Concerto for Solo Violin* (BÉLA BARTÓK),
It Wasn't God Who Made Honky Tonk Angels (VOCAL: KITTY KALLEN),
Siboney (UNKNOWN VOCAL), *Bee-Bop-a-Lula* (VOCAL: THE EVERLY BROTHERS),
excerpts from the score to *The Devil is a Woman* (PARAMOUNT, 1935) and
the soundtrack of *Ali Baba and the Forty Thieves* (UNIVERSAL, 1944). [2]

FRANCIS FRANCINE

Actress Maria Montez

AT ONCE PRIMITIVE AND SOPHISTICATED, HILARIOUS AND POIGNANT, spontaneous and studied, frenzied and languid, crude and delicate, avant and nostalgic, gritty and fanciful, fresh and faded, innocent and jaded, high and low, raw and cooked, underground and camp, black and white and white-on-white, composed and decomposed, richly perverse and gloriously impoverished, *Flaming Creatures* was something new under the sun. Had Jack Smith produced nothing other than this amazing artifact, he would still rank among the great visionaries of American film.

Flaming Creatures PROPOSED AN ENTIRELY NEW FORM OF cine-glamour—one that owed everything and nothing to Hollywood's. This discontinuous, 42-minute succession of "exotic" tableaux, served with a rich stew of (mainly) dated pop music, is a cross between Josef von Sternberg at his most studiedly artistic and a delirious home-movie of a transvestite bacchanal— except that "transvestite" is not precisely the word for Smith's gang of Arabian odalisques, Spanish dancers, blonde vampires, and sultry beatniks (half naked, some actual women). Nor would Sternberg have had the radically pragmatic aesthetic daring to use grossly outdated black-and-white film stock and thus give his images the flickering ethereality of a world half-consumed in the heat of its own desire.

Flaming Creatures
frame enlargement

A BURST OF THRILLING, PSEUDO-ORIENTAL PAGEANT MUSIC and a mysterious silvery screen: *Flaming Creatures* begins with an oblique evocation of Jack Smith's muse, the actress Maria Montez. The film's leisurely credit sequence is set to a three-and-a-half minute chunk of soundtrack lifted from the 1944 Montez vehicle *Ali Baba and the Forty Thieves*, replete with sonorous gongs and portentous drum rolls, and the hissed promise that "Today... Ali Baba comes today!" Ali Baba comes today! As in the Montez movie, as in all movies perhaps, there a sense of anticipatory tumult in the harem that, like all harems, implies the possibility of unlimited erotic pleasures—a feminine (or at least unmasculine), polysexual, polymorphous perversity. [3]

AMID LIGHT-STRUCK CLOSE-UPS OF PUCKERED MOUTHS, wagging tongues, and—without warning—a fondled penis, a variety of creatures rear up before the ornately lettered credits, rendering these titles even more difficult to read. Performers dart back and forth. A masked man, burly and bare-chested, enfolds a woman in his cloak and ducks out of camera range in reference to a similar move in Sternberg's *Shanghai Gesture*, thus revealing the barely decipherable cast names for the third time.

FALSE STARTS ARE ONE OF *Flaming Creatures's* RECURRING formal devices. Having playfully delayed the action through the extension of the credits, Smith cuts to a middle shot of his star Francis Francine in brocaded turban and matching white gown rapturously sniffing a lily. A somewhat longer shot introduces Delicious Dolores, a dark and zoftig young woman in a clingy black slip and floppy hat (SHEILA BICK), who is leaning back, hand on her head, before the movie's single backdrop—a Whistleresque painting of an outsized white vase containing a generous sprig of what could be almond blossoms.

3 The harem, as Malek Alloula notes, "is an erotic universe in which there are no men."

This lack of the phallus is eloquently symbolized by the two figures of the High Lord, who can neither enjoy all the women in his seraglio nor satisfy them, and of the eunuchs, who are the absolute negation of the male principle.

The Colonial Harem, trans. Myrna Godzich and Wlad Godzich (MINNEAPOLIS: UNIVERSITY OF MINNESOTA PRESS, 1986), P.96.

While few commentators on *Flaming Creatures* have failed to note the absence of male tumescence, Parker Tyler pushed the analysis of what actually happens on screen, noting that "that the drag act of presumably homosexual males is a strangely static and narcissistic routine as well as a sort of atavistic homage to the female."

Instead of the homosexual orgy we find in [Luchino Visconti's] The Damned and [Kenneth Anger's] Scorpio Rising— both of these oriented to male militarism, both finally excluding women altogether—Smith's peculiar transvestite cosmetic concerns flirtation between males in drag that turns into flirtation with a real woman and finally her rape by cunnilingus.

Screening the Sexes: Homosexuality in the Movies (NEW YORK: HOLT, RINEHART AND WINSTON, 1972), P.237. No participant in *Flaming Creatures* has verified Tyler's parenthetical assertion that the film includes a drag cameo by Smith himself.

11

A RECORDING OF MOVIE INGÉNUE DEANNA DURBIN TRILLING THE popular rumba *Amapola (Pretty Little Poppy)* provides accompaniment for Dolores's slow shimmy, her exposed back and ample backside turned to the camera. Francine waves and enters the frame. Suddenly ladylike, the pair flutter their fans, air kiss, and insincerely pinch each other's cheeks, turning away and back in synchronized disdain: which of the two is the song's "dainty little flower"?

Flaming Creatures
frame enlargement
(SHEILA BICK, right)

THE SONG'S END HERALDS WHAT SMITH'S JOURNALS TERM THE Smirching Sequence. Overhead shots showcase various creatures—including Francine, Dolores, and (in one of several manifestations) skinny, angular Joel Markman, here wearing a false nose and a ragged negligee—as they apply lipstick, sometimes in close-up, to the accompaniment of a convincing mock radio advertisement, complete with corny music, for a "new heart-shaped lipstick [that] shapes your lips as you color them." The illusion of an actual commercial is, however, shattered when the voice of Smith himself interrupts the genteel pitch-artist (FRANCIS FRANCINE) to wonder, "Is there a lipstick that doesn't come off when you suck cocks?" [4]

Flaming Creatures
frame enlargement

[4] The sequence suggests a bawdy variation on the "Stay-Put" lipstick campaign featured in Frank Tashlin's 1957 *Will Success Spoil Rock Hudson*—a movie Smith is unlikely to have seen or at least to admit having seen. "Even I detest the flix of the '50s," he parenthetically remarks in "The Perfect Filmic Appositeness of Maria Montez." *Wait For Me at the Bottom of the Pool: The Writings of Jack Smith*, ed. J. Hoberman and Edward Leffingwell (LONDON: SERPENT'S TAIL, 1997) P.33.

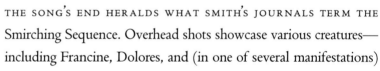

THIS QUESTION AND FRANCINE'S PRIM ANSWER ("INDELIBLE lipstick") precipitate a festive montage of hairy legs, waving penises, and rolling eyes. The background music continues, punctuated by the sound of amplified lip-smacks. All manner of unshaven mugs (photographed on a variety of film stocks) are seen, heads thrown back, studiously painting their smirched lips. Markman is concentrating with such intensity that he doesn't seem to notice the cock that coyly peeks over his shoulder. A brief tableau of half-naked bodies is followed by a somewhat longer shot of creatures collapsing in slow motion. After a static composition carefully framed to present the sole of someone's dirty foot, Francine is reintro-duced in close-up, glaring at the camera as the high-pitched Japanese ballad, *China Nights*, wells up on the track. [5]

The words to the song may be translated as follows:

China night, O China night:
Lights of the harbor, violet night,
The sound of strings on the ship of dreams.
I can't forget China night, night of dreams.
China night, O China night:
The lanterns swaying in the willows.
A Chinese girl with a red birdcage.
Inconsolable love song:
China night, night of dreams.

NEITHER SOLEMN NOR PRURIENT, *Flaming Creatures* MAKES a travesty of the sexual urge. In a paroxysm of jealousy or lust, Francine begins chasing Dolores. The cartoon quality of this undercranked (hence fast and blurry) pursuit is accentuated by its being staged and cut to suggest several impossible vectors as the rival stars pass back and forth before the great vase. At last, Francine seizes Dolores from behind and hurls her to the ground. Dolores cries out or, perhaps, she only pretends to. Faintly dubbed screams are heard as her breast, rendered even more generous by the camera's proximity, bounces out of her gown. As a kind of visual joke, Smith here inserts a close-up in which Dolores more decorously undoes her strap, then cuts back as she is ravished by a horde of creatures.

[5] *China Nights*, taken from a 78 rpm record supplied by the ex-merchant marine Arnold Rockwood, is the title song from the 1940 Japanese movie— one of several "Chinese continental friendship films" starring Yoshiko Yamaguchi, a.k.a. Li Xianglang, an actress born to a Japanese family in Manchuria, and thus perfectly bilingual. (In *China Night*, she typically plays a poor Chinese girl who initially hates the Japanese for killing her family but who nevertheless falls in love with a Japanese sailor.)

Like *Flaming Creatures*, *China Night* includes the bolero *Siboney*. Very likely, they are the only films in the history of cinema to contain both. The movie and the song were hits both in Japan and Japanese-occupied Shanghai. Brought to trial after the war, Yamaguchi survived to continue her career in Japan. She appeared in Samuel Fuller's 1956 *House of Bamboo* as Shirley Yamaguchi and was for many years a member of the Japanese Diet.

Flaming Creatures
frame enlargement
(JOEL MARKMAN, right)

As *China Nights* DISAPPEARS MID-PHRASE, THE CACOPHONOUS shrieks grow louder, mixing with an ominous thunder roll. The glass-paneled black lantern, another touch of Japonisme that dresses the otherwise austere set, begins to sway as if in the first tremors of an earthquake. Dolores struggles. She beats her fan on the gang of creatures now pinning her down, jiggling her breasts, poking their noses into her armpit, and otherwise exploring her person. Close examination of the footage reveals this sequence to have been assembled from at least three different shooting sessions—none involving more than four or five performers—but Dolores may even be screaming in earnest as her gown hikes up and the masked man of the credits (ARNOLD ROCKWOOD) slithers forward on his stomach to work his head between her thighs.

Journal notes,
Jack Smith, 1962.

Flaming Creatures
frame sequence
(JOEL MARKMAN)

ORGY TIME! AT THIS POINT, APPROXIMATELY HALFWAY THROUGH the movie, the overhead camera begins to participate, flailing over a tangle of writhing bodies. A second creature—a skinny male with a black wig and tatty slip—is held down beside Dolores and, feigning a campy panic, similarly ravished. The camera shakes; the earth moves; the lantern sways precipitously. Plaster dust cascades over the entwined creatures. Any single frame of the sequence is a dense arrangement of eyes, legs, hands, and genitalia. By way of a climax, Smith contrives a hyper-kinetic close-up of one creature's furtive attempt to lick another's toe. The debris seems real enough although, as David Packman has observed, the persistent disembodied screams suggest the "grisly effect" of a Coney Island spook house. [6]

ABRUPTLY, THERE IS SILENCE. THE ORGY IS SPENT. DOLORES staggers dramatically to her feet, accompanied by Béla Bartók's *Concerto for Solo Violin*, and promptly swoons backwards into the solicitous arms of the lithe and smiling Fascinating Woman (JUDITH MALINA), who wears pearls around her neck and has a flower clenched between her teeth. Petals rain upon the women as they kiss. A veil drifts idly in the breeze. For several long minutes, the camera considers the empty space and a fly crawling on the wall.

PRESENTLY, AS IF IN RESPONSE TO KITTY KALLEN'S PLAINTIVE declaration that *It Wasn't God Who Made Honky Tonk Angels*, a wooden coffin is seen to open and Our Lady of the Docks (JOEL MARKMAN), a bewigged transvestite vampire clutching a lily in each hand, awakes and emerges. Picking her way through the wreckage—which includes the fallen lantern—and prowling among the comatose creatures, Our Lady kneels over Francis Francine's neck to feast. She attacks her victim, rolling her eyes back in sated delight. Church bells toll. Eyes open in extreme close-up. Then, Our Lady lifts her dress and idly plays with her penis. [7]

6 "Jack Smith's *Flaming Creatures*: With the Tweak of an Eyebrow," *Film Culture* NO. 63–64 (1977) PP. 51–56.

7 Both Ken Kelman and P. Adams Sitney refer to Our Lady as "Marilyn Monroe." The allusion is appropriate in that Monroe was found dead on August 5, 1962, soon after Smith began shooting *Flaming Creatures*. In his notes, however, Smith links this figure to the fallen '40s star Veronica Lake: "A coffin on the set—Veronica Lake comes out—petals on lid disappear. She sucks Frankie Dry & they get up & two step together which turns into a production number."

Flaming Creatures
frame enlargements
(SHEILA BICK, left;
FRANCIS FRANCINE, right)

THIS RESURGENCE OF CARNAL INTEREST, ACCOMPANIED BY the genteel strains of the Cuban bolero *Siboney*, another 1930s standard, has a restorative effect. The creatures rise. The seraglio stages a celebration. Our Lady foxtrots with Francine—charmingly, neither seems certain which one of them should lead. This sequence, which, at seven minutes, is the movie's longest, is extensively edited and certainly combines several shooting sessions. As the camera whirls overhead, Our Lady can be seen dancing with at least two other people—one, the poet Ed Marshall, the other, an actual woman. Both are wearing Francine's distinctive turban and matching dress. The costume, as Smith often said, was the character. The actor only brings it to life.

LIKE A BUSBY BERKELEY MUSICAL, *Flaming Creatures* ENDS with an extended series of ensemble and solo dance numbers. Here, as throughout, the participants are cropped by Smith's handheld camera in unexpected ways. A sailor, apparently picked up that day and brought to the set, looks on bemused as a creature in a flat-brimmed hat and blackface (PIERO HELICZER) skips from side to side in a sort of capering hornpipe. Our Lady appears transfixed by a lily. The camera, similarly fascinated, investigates an armpit. Then, with a blast of bullfight music, and after one false start, the regal, giggling Spanish Girl (MARIO MONTEZ) twirls across the set.

Flaming Creatures
frame enlargement
(FRANCIS FRANCINE)

Flaming Creatures
frame enlargement
(MARIAN ZAZEELA, center
ANGUS MACLISE, right)

AS EXCERPTS FROM THE SOUNDTRACK OF STERNBERG'S *The Devil is a Woman* insinuate themselves into a mix of *Siboney* and an Italian aria, the screen is packed with all manner of dancing creatures, dappled by moving shadows and cascading streamers to suggest the Mardi Gras revelers in Sternberg's campiest Dietrich vehicle. This cavorting is intercut with a mock Delacroix tableau displaying an impassive odalisque (MARIAN ZAZEELA), her arm languidly resting atop her head and one breast exposed. She is surrounded and cushioned by a cluster of mock Arabs (IRVING ROSENTHAL, ANGUS MACLISE, LAMONTE YOUNG), one of whom solemnly points to her nipple.

ENDING AS LEISURELY AS IT BEGAN, *Flaming Creatures* OFFERS several minutes of curtain calls. In poignant silence, the Spanish Girl spins like a dervish and Our Lady extravagantly smokes a cigarette. Then, one final surprise: an incongruous burst of the Everly Brother's version of the teen-anthem *Be-Bop-a-Lula* as a flurry of last-minute kisses and swoons gives way to a shot of a leg dangling a high-heeled pump, the image of Our Lady being groped, an inverted flower, the end title, and a final close-up of a jiggling breast.

[8] Smith's remarks on *Flaming Creatures* may be found in his interview with Sylvére Lotringer, "Uncle Fishook and the Sacred Baby Poo Poo of Art," *Wait For Me at the Bottom of the Pool* OP.CIT., PP.107, 112.

Flaming Creatures's gender confusion was further compounded by its early commentators. Smith told Ken Kelman that the movie's female star Sheila Bick was, in fact, a hermaphrodite. Kelman duly reported this in his review of *Flaming Creatures* ("SMITH MYTH," *Film Culture* NO. 29) and it has been repeated elsewhere. Similarly, Judith Malina, who wears a masculine blond wig from the Living Theater production of William Carlos Williams's *Many Loves*, was mistakenly described by P. Adams Sitney as a transvestite.

SMITH LATER REFERRED TO *Flaming Creatures* AS A COMEDY SET IN A "HAUNTED MOVIE studio" and, in an undated draft of a letter to *The Village Voice*, explained that he "used transvestites in *Creatures* because of the visual comedy."

The film was as complete as possible a collection of the funniest and hopefully hilarious things I knew at that time... I should have added tapes of the 1st few audiences. I had read that Mack Sennet [sic] and others of that time designed their films to see if they could produce a continuous bellylaugh... [8]

17

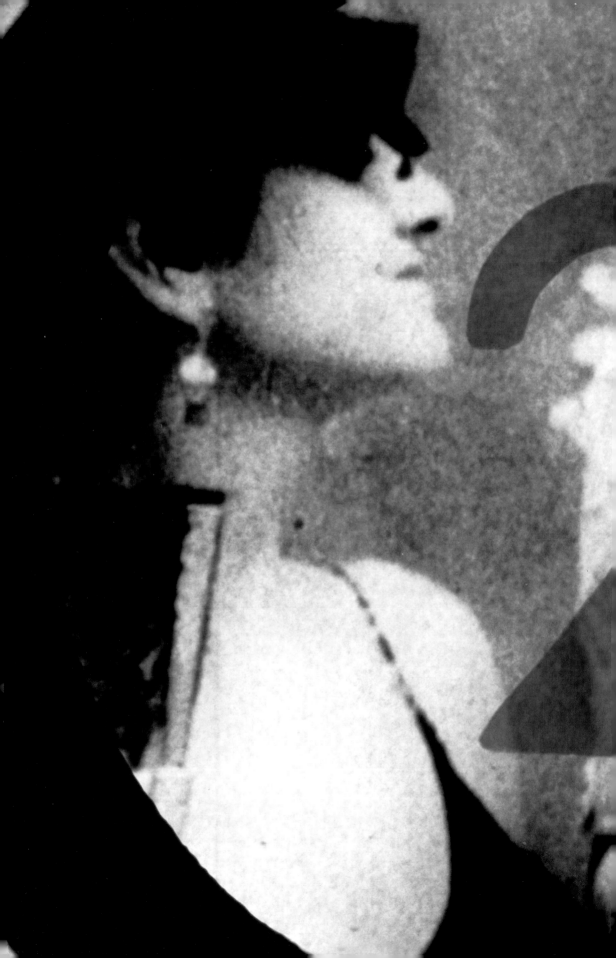

Making Flaming Creatures
Up on the Roof

Flaming Creatures
frame enlargement
(SHEILA BICK, left;
FRANCIS FRANCINE, right)

SHORTLY BEFORE HE BEGAN SHOOTING *Flaming Creatures*, Jack Smith purchased the ledger that would serve as his journal from mid 1962 through mid 1963, inscribing the opening page THIS IS A JOURNAL WITH ENDLESS PAGES. En face (beneath the rubric A MILLION TONS OF SHIT) is a list of things to do and people to contact. These include the notes "Call Von Sternberg" and "Eulogy to M. Montez. Why does no one remember her pix." [1]

CONSEQUENTLY EXPLICATING *Flaming Creatures* EVEN AS HE produced it, Smith articulated his film aesthetic in two early essays, "The Perfect Filmic Appositeness of Maria Montez" and "Belated Appreciation of V.S."—the first, his impassioned celebration of the much ridiculed 1940s movie star Maria Montez; the second, an appreciation of the visual poetry and unconscious transvestism in the movies Josef von Sternberg made with Marlene Dietrich. Both were originally published in *Film Culture*. [2]

SMITH'S CHAMPIONING OF STERNBERG AND MONTEZ MIGHT be considered manifestations of the sensibility that would soon be called camp were Smith's notions not so serious. As P. Adams Sitney would be the first to observe, *Flaming Creatures* made manifest what Smith found "implicated in Maria Montez and von Sternberg's films, and without the interference of a plot. What he brings to the fore is what has been latent in those films—visual texture, androgynous sexual presence, exotic locations." [3]

[1] The brainchild of producer Walter Wanger, albeit inspired by the success of Michael Powell's 1940 *Thief of Baghdad, Arabian Nights* (1943) was Universal's first all-color feature as well as the first of the six exotic vehicles Maria Montez made for the studio, mostly with Jon Hall and Sabu. In addition to its plenitude of harem beauties, the movie boasted the world's largest bathtub, rimmed with goatskins. Even before *Arabian Nights* broke opening day records, Montez signed to star in two follow-up sarong pictures, *White Savage* and *Cobra Woman* (both 1944). Earning nearly two million dollars, *Arabian Nights* proved to be Wanger's most financially successful film thus far. By 1944, he ranked just below Louis B. Mayer as the second highest paid man in Hollywood while Montez was the most popular player under Universal contract—the much-publicized "Queen of Technicolor."

[2] The two essays are reprinted in *Wait for Me at the Bottom of the Pool: The Writings of Jack Smith*, ed. J. Hoberman and Edward Leffingwell (LONDON: SERPENT'S TAIL, 1997).

[3] *Visionary Film: The American Avant-Garde 1943–1978*, second edition (NEW YORK: OXFORD UNIVERSITY PRESS, 1979), P.353.

MONTEZ VEHICLES AND STERNBERG/DIETRICH COLLABORATIONS further suggested a particular mode of being. The title *Blonde Cobra*, used by Ken Jacobs for his 1963 portrait of Smith, combines Dietrich's *Blonde Venus* with Montez's *Cobra Woman* and was invented by Smith as a name for the diva he might play himself. Dietrich, Smith wrote, was Sternberg's own "visual projection—a brilliant transvestite in a world of delirious unreal adventures." Smith would tell Marian Zazeela, his most important model during the 1961–62 making of *The Beautiful Book*, that he considered himself a Sternberg to her Dietrich. [4]

[4] Lawrence Rinder, "Anywhere Out of the World: The Photography of Jack Smith," *Jack Smith: Flaming Creature—His Amazing Life and Times*, ed. Edward Leffingwell (LONDON: SERPENT'S TAIL/PS I MUSEUM, 1997), P.144.

BUT, IF DIETRICH WAS STERNBERG'S PROJECTION, MARIA MONTEZ had, even more miraculously, managed to project her own world: Montezland. "The Perfect Filmic Appositeness of Maria Montez" begins with the declaration that "at least in America a Maria Montez could believe she was the Cobra woman, the Siren of Atlantis, Scheherazade, etc. She believed and thereby made the people who went to her movies believe." According to Ronald Tavel, the other leading Montez theorist of the early '60s Lower East Side, Smith not only considered Montez to be "the most perfect object" for a movie camera to consider, but imagined that the force of the star's imagination exerted itself upon the entire crew. [5]

[5] Ronald Tavel, unpublished interview with J. Hoberman and Callie Angell (8/24/94). Tavel has several times written on Smith and Montez. See his "Maria Montez: Anima of an Antedeluvian World," *Jack Smith: Flaming Creature*, OP.CIT., as well as his dossier on the Theatre of the Ridiculous, *Tri-Quarterly 6* (1967), PP.93–109.

Smith's sense of Montez was borne out by Robert Siodmak, who told John Russell Taylor in an interview published in *Sight and Sound* (SUMMER-AUTUMN 1959), that while the star "couldn't act from here to there..."

She was a great personality and believed completely in her roles: if she was to play a princess you had to treat her like one all through lunch, but if she was a slave-girl you could kick her around anyhow and she wouldn't object—method acting before its time, you might say (P.181).

While reviewer Bosley Crowther complained that Montez played "the beauteous dancer with the hauteur of a tired nightclub showgirl" (*New York Times*, 12/25/42), other critics seem to have understood *Arabian Nights* as something like camp. Noting that this material "used to be played straight in Doug Fairbank's day," *P.M*'s John T. McManus called it "the gaudiest and most cynical transformation of a classic since the Ritz Brothers played *The Three Musketeers*." Alton Cooke remarked in *The New York World-Telegram* on the whistling, hooting, wisecracking spectators. "It was just about the wildest audience since the time a gang of youngsters was hired to turn hoodlum and stage a riot for Benny Goodman around the Paramount." (*Arabian Nights* CLIPPINGS, NEW YORK PUBLIC LIBRARY, LIBRARY OF THE PERFORMING ARTS.)

6 *The Films of Josef von Sternberg* (NEW YORK: MUSEUM OF MODERN ART, 1966), PP.41–42.

7 "Belated Appreciation of V.S.," *Wait for Me*, OP.CIT., P.42.

In his journal, Smith maintains that, for *The Devil is a Woman*,

Von Sternberg got Dos Passos to write the worst dialogue of 1936. He constructed ludicrous, exaggerated Hollywood Nutty Spanish sets, made a wonderful moldy-corny melodamatic atmosphere in which Dietrich could wax deliriously hammy. He turned melodrama upon itself and came up with a true personal fantasy. This was no Spain, even of the inept Hollyood imitation style—this was layer over layer of clutter, extras in rented costumes, light and shadow as it never existed in nature or even art up to this point, costumes that Dietrich must have had difficulty standing up in, in short a perfect artistic Spain...

"The Perfect Filmic Appositeness of Maria Montez," *Wait for Me*, OP.CIT., P.35.

In his lecture "The Perfect Queer Appositeness of Jack Smith" (9/24/99; STEIRISCHER HERBST, GRAZ, AUSTRIA), Jerry Tartaglia called these human slips the "focal points" of Smith's films.

"They are moments of rupture in the fabric of the cinematic illusion."

The viewer is slapped in the face and reminded of the illusionary nature of the film. But Jack was not content to allow for randomly occurring slips and ruptures. He took this a few steps further. He created conditions in which the ruptures were bound to occur during the shooting. Beverly Grant's performance

22

with the live cobra in Normal Love, the Mermaid and the Werewolf falling into the mud, the creatures dancing with the frightened cows—all these scenes were brought about because Jack created the conditions in which the confluence of actors, sets, costumes, and impossible actions bring about "accidents" which move the viewer out of the state of reverie and into an alienated state of awareness.

For a discussion of Smith's view of Montez in the context of surrealist film aesthetics see my "Bad Movies," *Vulgar Modernism: Writing on Movies and Other Media* (TEMPLE UNIVERSITY PRESS: PHILADELPHIA, 1991) and "Jack Smith: Bagdada and Lobsterrealism," *Wait for Me*, OP.CIT.

AS THE CREDIT SEQUENCE OF *Flaming Creatures* QUOTES A moment from Sternberg's *Shanghai Gesture*, so its "Carnival of Ecstasy" evokes what Sternberg called *The Devil is a Woman*'s "riotous carnival." Writing on this "transfigured tinsel tradition" in his 1966 Museum of Modern Art monograph, Andrew Sarris noted with amazement "how little space Sternberg requires to evoke an empire, and how little time to evoke an era. The sheer economy of the director's mise-en-scene has seldom been appreciated..." Sternberg's decor, Sarris wrote, was "not the meaningless background of the drama, but its very subject, peering through nets, veils, screens, shutters, bars, cages, mists, flowers, and fabrics to tantalize the male with fantasies of the female." 6

THE SAME MIGHT BE SAID FOR SMITH, WHO GOES EVEN further than Sarris, citing *The Devil is a Woman* to include actors in Sternberg's mise-en-scene: "The script says Count so and so (in *Devil is a Woman*) is a weak character. The plot piles up situation after situation—but needlessly—Sternberg graphically illustrates this by using a tired actor [LIONEL ATWILL] giving a bad performance." The notion of a bad, and hence triumphantly revealing, performance is crucial to Smith's appreciation of Montez and, indeed, his entire aesthetic. "In my movies, I know that I prefer non-actor stars to 'convincing' actor-stars— only a personality that exposes itself—if through moldiness (human slips can convince me—in movies) and I was very convinced by Maria Montez in her particular case of her great beauty and integrity." 7

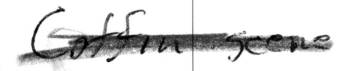

IN HIS 1962–63 JOURNAL, SMITH MADE A FEW NOTES FOR A "Maria Montez Flic":

> *The Plaster Movie Studio broods in a deep shadow, obscured by scaffolding... Director prays to Miss Montez. They use a corpse as leading lady. Record them fluffing their lines, freudian slips—complaining—asking director for pins, being retouched by makeup woman, staring lost into mirrors.*

THIS SCENARIO WAS EVENTUALLY REALIZED NOT AS A MOVIE but by the written piece "The Memoirs of Maria Montez." [8]

[8] "Perfect Filmic Appositeness," *Wait for Me*, OP.CIT., PP. 37–39.

MONTEZ WAS ONLY THE MOST IMPORTANT OF SMITH'S STARS. He collected images of George Chakiris and, according to Tavel, was fascinated by Gale Sondergaard. Smith's interest had nothing to do with Sondergaard's political history—like her husband Herbert Biberman, one of the Hollywood Ten, she was blacklisted —and everything to do with her portrayal of the charmingly malevolent Spider Woman in two Sherlock Holmes mysteries. Tavel recalls that, excited to learn that Sondergaard would be appearing in a one-woman off-Broadway show during the autumn of 1965, Smith went backstage on opening night to invite the actress to appear in one of his movies. She declined. [9]

[9] Tavel interview, OP.CIT.

Journal notes, Jack Smith, 1962.

Untitled "plastique,"
Jack Smith, circa 1962.
(MARIO MONTEZ, center;
ARNOLD ROCKWELL, right)

Flaming Creatures WAS INITIALLY CONCEIVED AS A VEHICLE FOR MARIAN ZAZEELA. However, Zazeela's meeting and subsequent involvement with the composer LaMonte Young precluded her participation: "I had to spend night and day with LaMonte," she later explained. [10]

THUS, "LA GRAN ESTRELLA Maria [sic] Zazeela," as she is known in Smith's journal, was replaced by another Lower East Side ingénue, Sheila Bick, the wife of Zazeela's high school boyfriend. The musician and future-filmmaker Tony Conrad, a disciple of Young's who had just graduated from Harvard, was invited to stay at Zazeela's now-vacated East 9TH Street studio. There, in the early summer of 1962, he discovered Smith installed and in the process of assembling *The Beautiful Book*, a collection of photographs which Conrad deemed "some kind of bizarre, contemptible New York art pornography." [11]

BY HIS OWN ACCOUNT, CONRAD INITIALLY REGARDED HIS eccentric roommate with benign contempt.

[10] Marian Zazeela, unpublished interview with Edward Leffingwell (FEBRUARY 1996). Introduced to Smith by writer Irving Rosenthal, in late fall 1961, Zazeela, then a young painter, became the most important female model in the series of photography sessions Smith staged weekends from late 1961 through June 1962 at his Lower East Side apartment—tableaux that featured many subsequent participants in *Flaming Creatures*, including Francis Francine, Mario Montez, Joel Markman, Ronald Tavel, and David Gurin.

[11] Tony Conrad in David Reisman, "In the Grip of the Lobster: Jack Smith Remembered," *Millennium Film Journal* NO. 23/24 (WINTER 1990–91), P.63.

KISSES

Untitled "plastique,"
Jack Smith, circa 1962.
(MARIAN ZAZEELA, left;
MARIO MONTEZ, right)

I found Jack one day working on a gigantic grey painting of a vase of flowers, maybe nine feet square. "How marvelous," thought I, ironically, "a vase of flowers." "Oh, uh, Jack, what is this?" Jack said, "It's the set for my new movie." [12]

12 Conrad, Reisman, OP.CIT., P.63.

ALTHOUGH "STILL AT THIS POINT QUITE UNIMPRESSED," Conrad nevertheless offered to help Smith transport the painting to his movie's location, schlepping it some fifteen blocks downtown to the leaky, tar-paper roof of the Windsor Theater at 412 Grand Street, where *Flaming Creatures* was staged and shot over the course of eight or so weekend afternoons throughout the late summer and early fall.

HAVING ESTABLISHED THE CHARLES THEATER ON AVENUE B AS an ongoing concern, owner Walter Langsford had acquired the venerable Windsor (said to be the city's oldest extant movie house) with an eye to expanding his Lower East Side exhibition empire. Photographer-filmmaker Richard Preston, who produced some animated collage trailers for the Charles, took the unfinished loft above the theater as his studio. This space, which

13 Richard Preston, unpublished interview with J.H. (4/30/96).

overlooked and opened onto the Windsor's roof, served as *Flaming Creatures*'s dressing room and prop department, as well as providing a physical support for the painted backdrop Conrad helped carry to the set. [13]

14 Conrad, Reisman, OP.CIT., P.64. Tony Conrad, unpublished interview with J.H. (5/10/96).

ON HIS FIRST VISIT TO THE WINDSOR ROOF, CONRAD discovered that "there were lots of weird substances being consumed and strange people arriving on the scene."

And boy, was I surprised when it turned out that people took three hours to put on their makeup; I was very more surprised when people took several more hours to put on their costumes.

(CONRAD'S ULTIMATE SURPRISE CAME WHEN, AFTER assigning him a dress to wear, Smith "ripped it down the back to expose my ass and turned my back to the camera.") [14]

The Windsor Theater, 412 Grand Street, circa 1939.

WHEN, IN "THE PERFECT FILMIC APPOSITENESS OF MARIA MONTEZ," Smith wrote that film is "a place where it is possible to clown, to pose, to act out fantasies, to not be seen while one gives (Movie sets are sheltered, exclusive places where nobody who doesn't belong can go)," he was, in a sense, describing the making of *Flaming Creatures*. The three-story Windsor was flanked by higher buildings, which, as old-law tenements, had no side windows. Thus, the lengthy preparations and riotous goings-on involved in the production of the movie would only have been visible from an adjacent roof, one story up. Preston remembers sporadic complaints, but no actual disturbances. [15]

15 Preston, OP.CIT.

NORMAN SOLOMON'S PRODUCTION PHOTOGRAPHS REVEAL *Flaming Creatures*'s sheltered, if not shaded, open-air set to be a secluded and surprisingly small space—marked by a painter's drop cloth estimated by one participant as 10x14 feet—not unlike the courtyard used by Ken Jacobs for *Star Spangled to Death*. A ladder, supported at a slight angle by a seven-foot stepladder and the roof of Preston's loft, provided a hook for the glass lantern and served as a rickety catwalk for overhead shooting. Smith not only directed *Flaming Creatures* but, using available light (if not a light meter), filmed the action himself. His sole credit is "Photographer" and he can be seen, in one of the photos, holding Preston's 16mm, three-lens Bolex. [16]

Flaming Creatures WAS SHOT ON A VARIETY OF BLACK-AND-white reversal film stocks, including such exotic brands as Agfa-Ferrania and Dupont, stolen from the outdated film bin at Camera Barn. (According to Conrad, Smith made particular use of Perutz Tropical film—a German stock designed for shooting at high temperatures—because, thanks to its counter location, it was the easiest to shoplift.) Preston notes that the late-afternoon lack of direct sunlight contributed to the ethereal, distinctively low-contrast quality of imagery. [17]

CONRAD'S RECOLLECTIONS SUGGEST THAT THE LENGTHY "Carnival Ecstasy" sequence was, in fact, the first section of the film to be shot although, by all accounts, Smith took great care in preparing for each shooting session. Preston, an observing non-participant, was surprised at how "orderly" and "businesslike" the production actually was. Although he could not imagine a finished film emerging from such primitive conditions, he remembers being struck by the actors' "reverence" for Smith. [18]

[16] Conrad, unpublished OP.CIT. Preston, OP.CIT. The two rolls of 35mm film (color and black-and-white) shot by Norman Solomon on the *Flaming Creatures* set afford some indication of the space. Scenes shot on the afternoon Solomon was present include a version of the Orgy-Rape-Earthquake sequence (without Francis Francine) and possibly material for the Smirching Sequence.

[17] Conrad, unpublished OP.CIT. Preston, OP.CIT.

[18] Preston, OP.CIT. Various participants assumed Smith's direction was improvised and spontaneous. In fact, his journal notes are fairly detailed. *Flaming Creatures* was intended to open with a "Smirching Sequence: Marion [sic] & Francine applying lipstick." The scenario continues:

Marion and Francine pose about envying each others lips... F.F. grabs at M. The chase. Marion strikes with purse. the clinch. F.F. pulls out her tit. (E.Q. [earthquake] builds up)... C.U. of F.F. bouncing M's tit. Marion screaming & struggling. Final shot of many people holding M. down as F. blobbles her tit. F's erection under his dress.

With the exception of the final fillip and the substitution of Sheila Bick for Marian Zazeela, the final film plays much as written. The screams are written into the script as are the tolling bells that accompany "Marion's recovery." (There is, however, an unfilmed twist: "Mary [the part taken by Judith Malina in the movie] puts Marion on a camel and they ride off across the desert—Mary's burnoose flowing (chorus of religious music swells)."

27

RONALD TAVEL, WHO CROUCHED ON THE CATWALK POURING plaster dust down on the actors while Smith filmed the Rape-Earthquake-Orgy, cites the solemnity with which one of the women, most likely Sheila Bick, was filmed partially nude. Other participants remember an altogether more delirious environment. By Joan Adler's secondhand account, the Rape-Earthquake-Orgy was shot "in broiling sunlight."

> *With the set falling all over [the performers] high as kites,*
> *Jack pouring ceiling plaster all over them (a large chunk*
> *bruised Frankie, who got mad telling about those sufferings*
> *too) and careening dangerously above on some swinging,*
> *homemade contraption.* [19]

WHILE IT WOULD SURELY BE AN EXAGGERATION TO DESCRIBE *Flaming Creatures* as having been created in a state of stoned ecstasy, the participants were scarcely innocent of New York's still-underground drug culture. Marijuana, cocaine, and methamphetamine were at various times used on the set; indeed, Sheila Bick's husband (a chemist) was busted for cocaine manufacture at the time of the filming. [20]

[19] Ronald Tavel, unpublished interview with J.H. and Callie Angell (8/24/94). "On Location" in Stephen Dwoskin, *Film Is: The International Free Cinema* (WOODSTOCK NY: THE OVERLOOK PRESS, 1975), P.12. No participant in *Flaming Creatures* to whom I spoke supports Adler's suggestion that Jerry Jofen shot portions of the film. For all its visual tumult, the orgy sequence may have involved as few as five performers.

The source of this falling plaster may be deduced from an anecdote related by Walter Langsford during the course of a memorial held for Smith at P.S. 122 on October 16, 1989. Langsford recalled that *Flaming Creatures* was in production while he and a crew were renovating the Windsor below.

[Smith] went up on the roof with what equipment he had and what friends he had. And we went on about our business. Half an hour or so later we heard this tremendous crashing noise from the roof, and I ran up and Jack had a sledgehammer, and he was banging away at one of the main support beams.

(TRANSCRIPT COURTESY EDWARD LEFFINGWELL.)

In a journal entry dated August 11, Smith refers to "the incident on the Windsor Roof" and expresses an unfounded concern that Langsford may prevent subsequent filming. In September, Langsford and his partner Ed Stein announced plans to reopen Windsor as a sister theater to the Charles; both movie houses went dark the end of the year.

[20] Conrad, unpublished OP.CIT. Marian Zazeela and LaMonte Young, unpublished interview with J.H., July 1996. This may or may not be the drug bust at the Clinton Street apartment of Irwin and Sheila Bick that was reported in *The New York Mirror* as 'BEATS' PANIC, TOSS OUT DOPE KIT, BOP A COP. The clipping is undated, although

a brief item below, recounting an attempted rape on a Florida golf course, is dated April 27—which would mean that the police raid either preceded the start of the *Flaming Creatures* shoot by at least a month or else occurred two days before the movie had its public premiere at the Bleecker Street Cinema.

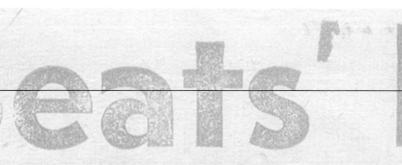

'Beats' Panic, Toss Out Dope Kit, Bop a Cop

By MIKE PEARL and HARRY OBER

Detectives who went to an East Side tenement looking for a burglar yesterday didn't find him, but their presence scared the "beat" tenants of a top-floor "pad" into tossing a breadbox out the window.

The breadbox hit someone in the street—a "fuzz." You know, like a cop, man. The box smashed on the sidewalk, spilling packets of heroin, hypodermic syringes, needles, eye-droppers—the works.

UP IN THE PAD—furnished mainly with a mattress, throw-pillows, bongo drums and non-objective paintings—was a refrigerator with no space wasted on food.

It held "hundreds of goofballs of at least 15 types, more needles, eyedroppers — enough 'junk' to last till October," said Detective Sgt. John Brennan, of the Clinton St. station.

An artist, Irwin Bick, 24, and his wife sheila, 26, a model, who occupied the flat at 6 Clinton St., were arrested as were three visiting friends.

The three were William Boss, 28, a poet, of 138 Wooster St.; Constance Knebel, 26, an actress, also of 138 Wooster St.; and Charles Hayden, 24, of 339 W. 87th St., a musician who said he plays "everything, man, but everything." All five are jobless.

A police car and squad car had pulled up in front of the building, sirens blasting in answer to a burglary alarm, which proved unfounded. Patrolman Thaddeus Kondos was standing near a car when passersby screamed as they saw the breadbox falling from the upper-floor window. Kondos looked up and ducked, but it grazed him.

THE DETECTIVES hustled to the top floor and at first couldn't get into the flat. It was only after the occupants heard a policeman being dispatched to the District Attorney's office for a search warrant that they opened up.

The search was conducted to music—way out jazz coming from a tape-recorder. The men needed slaves, and a pants press wouldn't have hurt any of them. Mrs. Bick was dressed like a square—in a dress, but no make-up. Miss Knebel made up for that with slacks about four sizes too small and a sweater four sizes too large.

Neighbors said the joint jumped with parties almost every night.

All five were charged with possession of narcotics, a felony, and the Bicks additionally with maintaining a place fo rtheir use. They will be arraigned in Felony Court this morning.

Woman Attacked On Golf Course

LAKELAND, Fla., April 27 (UPI).—A woman golfer, playing alone, was attacked by a naked man wearing a hood on the Cleveland Heights Country Club golf course.

The man tore off all the woman's clothes above the waist, but fled when her screams brought other golfers running to her aid. The attacker fled into a nearby swamp and bloodhounds were unable to follow his trail.

It was the second such attack on the course within a year.

HELP YOUR···t e e t h to last a lifetime. It can be d o n e, knowing the authoritative facts featured in "Mental Dental Drill…a health special in Sunday's Mirror Magazine. It's most interesting, and can save you and y o u r family anguish…and teeth!

Undated clipping, *The New York Mirror* (courtesy Norman Solomon)

21 Tavel, OP.CIT. Zazeela, unpublished OP.CIT. Smith's correspondence suggests some mild tension on the roof that afternoon:

> *Irving became overstimulated Sunday and said certain semi-tactless cracks in an attempt at ironic levity but they went over like lead balloon and caused Joel to walk off the set of* Flaming Creatures *and later when they were taking off their gowns there was an exchange of homo-waspishness between them.*

ACCORDING TO TAVEL, *Flaming Creatures* WAS ORIGINALLY to be called *Pasty Thighs and Moldy Midriffs*. (Alternate titles gleaned from Smith's journal include *Flaking Moldy Almond Petals*, *Moldy Rapture*, and *Horora Femina*.) By summer's end, the title was definitely *Flaming Creatures*. Zazeela, who painted the film's spidery credits, consented to pose for one sequence. In late September, after the Carnival of Ecstasy and Rape-Earthquake-Orgy scenes had been filmed, she arrived at the Windsor accompanied by LaMonte Young and Irving Rosenthal. 21

Rene - Kisses Joel - Francine on knees

Francine's hand on Joel's ~~croke~~

~~Francine~~ ~~Posing~~s

~~Francine potion lipstick~~

Titles
The last shot.
~~Coffin scene~~

~~More Lipstick~~ — B~~r~~

~~Close~~ ~~fucking~~.

Judith's shots.

~~Francine Posing~~

Lantern moving — high shot - (about Lantern)
Sheila posing surrounded by creatures Sheila DIFFUSED

Shooting notes,
Jack Smith, 1962

THE *Flaming Creatures* SHOOT EXTENDED WELL INTO OCTOBER. Judith Malina, the co-founder of the Living Theater, remembers filming her scene with Sheila Bick on the afternoon of Yom Kippur. Malina, fasting in observance of the Jewish holy day, maintains that Smith positioned the two actresses on "a heap of flower petals and garbage" with "absolutely no preparation." ("Jack shouted 'Pull out her booby. Push her tit in!' I pushed in her nipple as if it were a doorbell," is how Malina recalled Smith's direction, although their encounter seems hardly so violent. [22])

[22] Judith Malina, unpublished interview with J.H. (5/10/96)

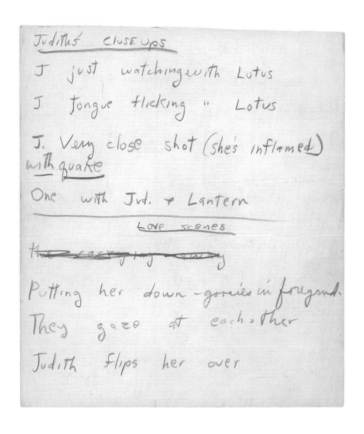

SMITH'S LETTER TO HIS FRIEND DAVID GURIN SUGGESTS THAT, a week or so later, *Flaming Creatures* was still in production:

> *Instead of finishing the movie according to the script I shot some pure psychotic footage of Sheila SINGING... singing mind you—I was reeling I was so zonked that morning behind that c... Now I spend my days wondering where to insert that footage.*

SMITH FURTHER NOTES THAT "THE MOVIE'S EXPENSES ARE mounting" and there was difficulty getting the footage processed: "We have to send it to Colorado to Stanley Brakhage." [23]

[23] The first portion of Smith's letter—written over two days but dated "who knows"—is published in *Wait for Me*, OP.CIT., P.164.

Brakhage, who was experienced in processing problematic footage, had a close working relationship with Western Cine-Lab in Denver. In a letter dated Halloween 1962, Smith wrote Gurin that, although *Flaming Creatures* was completely shot, "I've been waiting three weeks now for it to be sent to Colorado to be developed. Due to Dick Preston's farting around." *Flaming Creatures*'s total budget, Jonas Mekas would later report in *The Village Voice* (6/13/63), was $300. While this unverifiable figure was likely devoted to film processing, some went for props. Smith's October 6 letter to Gurin complains of being "doublecrossed by the funeral home turds" who charged him a "$10 rental for Joel's coffin."

THAT ONLY 15 MINUTES OF *Flaming Creatures* OUTTAKES are known to remain suggests a frugal shooting-ratio, all the more impressive in that Smith evidently filmed many crucial scenes without benefit of seeing his earlier rushes. Gregory Markopoulos would write that Smith needed only a week to cut *Flaming Creatures*. Given the density of the montage (and the other events of the fall, which included Smith's arrest for shoplifting), this seems unlikely. In any case, several months were required for the closely synchronized sound accompaniment that Conrad assembled on ¼-inch magnetic tape in the winter of 1962–63. [24]

SMITH SCREENED THE UNFINISHED *Flaming Creatures* FOR friends and associates throughout the winter, with one publicized benefit organized by Piero Heliczer's Dead Language Press at painter Jerry Jofen's cavernous West 20TH Street loft, which, among other things, had a reputation as a shooting gallery. [25]

NEWS OF THE MOVIE BROKE INTO PRINT IN MID-APRIL WHEN Jonas Mekas wrote in his *Village Voice* column that Smith had just completed "a great movie." *Flaming Creatures*, Mekas maintained,

> is so beautiful that I feel ashamed even to sit through the current Hollywood and European movies. I saw it privately and there is little hope that Smith's movie will ever reach the movie theatre screens. But I tell you, it is a most luxurious outpouring of imagination, of imagery, of poetry, of movie artistry, comparable only to the work of the greatest, like Von Sternberg. [26]

[24] Conrad, unpublished OP.CIT.

[25] A sometime visitor chez Jofen, P. Adams Sitney provided a vivid memoir in the May–June 1997 issue of the Anthology Film Archives calendar:

A cluttered, wildly messy series of large rooms one flight up from the street... It delivered the shock of another world. The railroad corridor led to an immense studio, heaped with monumental canvases, thick with overpainting and collage... [The sleeping quarters were] always filled with people, more women than men. Most of them seemed dangerous or desperate in my nineteen-year-old eyes. I came to imagine it alternately as a harem or shooting gallery... (N.P.)

Joan Adler describes the scene in similar terms, "On Location," OP.CIT., P.16.

[26] *Movie Journal: The Rise of a New American Cinema* (NEW YORK: COLLIER BOOKS, 1972), P.83.

Very close shot (she's inflamed
quote

NOT TWO WEEKS LATER AND ACCOMPANIED BY A SECOND version of Tony Conrad's taped soundtrack, a further revised *Flaming Creatures* received its theatrical premiere, midnight, April 29, 1963, at the Bleecker Street Cinema on a bill with *Blonde Cobra*. [27]

Flaming Creatures's DEFINITIVE VERSION MAY BE DATED TO midsummer. In early August, Mekas and Jacobs attended the Flaherty Film Seminar, an international documentary event held in Brattleboro, Vermont, toting prints of *Blonde Cobra* and *Flaming Creatures*. It was late before Mekas was able to get the movies on the projector. "Midnight screenings in Vermont!" he exclaimed to his readers. "My God, we felt like underground even at Flaherty's." (This expedition is documented in the last reel of Mekas's epic diary film *Lost, Lost, Lost*. [28])

Flaming Creatures WAS DISTRIBUTED BY THE FILM-MAKERS' Cooperative from 1963 through 1968. By the end of 1965, Smith had withdrawn the printing materials for both *Flaming Creatures* and the short *Overstimulated* from the Coop's safe-keeping, although it is unclear whether *Overstimulated* was actually ever in circulation.

SOME POINT IN THE LATE '60s, PERHAPS ANTICIPATING A licensing agreement with the new film division at Grove Press, Smith produced a "corrected" high contrast print of *Flaming Creatures*. The edited camera original was subsequently lost until miraculously discovered in 1978 by filmmaker Jerry Tartaglia among a mass of lab-discarded 16mm sound fill. [29]

[27] Conrad, unpublished, OP.CIT.

[28] Mekas, OP.CIT., P.95.

[29] Jerry Tartaglia, "Restoration and Slavery," *Jack Smith: Flaming Creature*, OP.CIT., P.208.

"Crimson Creatures"

The Case
Against
Flaming Creatures

Flaming Creatures frame enlargement
(SHEILA BICK, left
FRANCIS FRANCINE, center)

REVILED, BANNED, RIOTED OVER, *Flaming Creatures* IS THE ONLY American avant-garde film whose reception approximates the scandals that greeted *L'Age d'Or* or *Zero de Conduite*. It seems unfair that so light and playful a movie should bear so heavy a burden of notoriety—certainly Smith himself felt burned, bitterly complaining that his film, "designed as a comedy," had been transformed into "a sex issue of the Cocktail World." Yet, the tumult that *Flaming Creatures* occasioned is nearly as illuminating in its way as the movie itself. [1]

[1] Jack Smith, "Pink Flamingo formulas in focus," *The Village Voice* (7/19/73), p.69.

The Elgin theater began showing *Pink Flamingos* as a midnight attraction in March 1973; by mid-April, it was the talk of New York. Smith reviewed *Pink Flamingos* in *The Village Voice*, some four months into its run, although his notice served mainly as an opportunity to attack the two *Village Voice* movie critics, Jonas Mekas and Andrew Sarris.

Clearly, Smith recognized *Pink Flamingos* as akin to *Flaming Creatures*, praising Waters for the "nausea factor [he] seems uncannily to have built into the film, the excesses of which would be too revolting when described [in] the Breeze of Death style of Mekas and the secret media-maid peter patter of Sarris."

"They can eat shit"—in the words of the dialogue of one of the best scenes in *Pink Flamingos*, the speech in the opening of which is marked by a moronic quality that you know at any moment could erupt into filth. This moment is deliciously held back for a few seconds until "...you can eat shit..." line spews irrestibly from the lips of one of the film's two spectacular leading ladies. From that moment on the dialogue becomes a gilded torrent of filth, the colors become more and more garish as the story unfolds of a clash, that results in a trailer-burning, between two families, each in the thrall of a super-bitch in the family who opposes the other over the issue of which of them is the world's filthiest woman. This issue, hardly resolved by the trailer burning, is at last settled by the one known as Divine, a queen (whose family trailer it was) who sticks her fingers into a fresh pile of her dog's shit on the sidewalk and licks it off in the film's closing moments.

"Queer?" Smith concluded. "I think such antics seem virile and wholesome when compared with the unmanly activities of the publicity dykes of Atlantis seemingly bursting with film chatter who really are only pyorrheal piranhas."

(For an account of Waters's early career and development in the context of the New York underground, see Stefan Brecht, *Queer Theatre* (FRANKFURT AM MAIN: SUHRKAMP VERLAG, 1978), pp.137–56, and J. Hoberman and Jonathan Rosenbaum, *Midnight Movies* (NEW YORK: HARPER & ROW, 1983), pp.136–73.

Flaming Creatures HAD ITS THEATRICAL PREMIERE AT midnight, April 29, 1963, at the Bleecker Street Cinema, and there its vicissitudes—and those of the underground—began. For starters, all Underground Midnights at the Bleecker were cancelled. According to Mekas, the theater managers, Marshall Lewis and Rudy Franchi, complained that the "low quality of the underground" was ruining the Bleecker's reputation. [2]

[2] *Midnight Movies,* OP. CIT., P.51.

RESPONDING IN *The Village Voice*, MEKAS ISSUED A manifesto on the "Baudelairean Cinema," citing *Flaming Creatures, The Queen of Sheba Meets the Atom Man, Blonde Cobra,* and *Little Stabs at Happiness* as the four movies making up "the real revolution in cinema today." These movies, he declared,

> ...are illuminating and opening up sensibilities and experiences never before recorded in the American arts; a content which Baudelaire, the Marquis de Sade, and Rimbaud gave to world literature a century ago and which [William] Burroughs gave to American literature three years ago. It is a world of flowers of evil, of illuminations, of torn and tortured flesh; a poetry which is at once beautiful and terrible, good and evil, delicate and dirty. A thing that may scare an average viewer is that this cinema is treading on the very edge of perversity. These artists are without inhibitions, sexual or any other kind... There is now a cinema for the few, too terrible and too "decadent" for an "average" man in any organized culture. [3]

[3] Jonas Mekas, *Movie Journal: The Rise of a New American Cinema* (NEW YORK: COLLIER BOOKS, 1972), PP.85–86.

[4] Jonas Mekas, "Experimental Film Producers Protest Arbitrary Action of New York Labs," *Film World and AV News Magazine* (SEPTEMBER 1963).

AS IF IN CONFIRMATION, MEKAS SUBSEQUENTLY NOTED IN the *Voice* that no film laboratory would print *Flaming Creatures*; the next issue of *Film World and AV News Magazine* elaborated his complaint that New York City labs were routinely destroying footage found to have images of nudes. [4]

THAT SUMMER, MEKAS RELOCATED HIS UNDERGROUND screenings to the Gramercy Arts, a small theater in the East 20s, off Lexington Avenue. *Flaming Creatures*'s first reviews appeared in the autumn. Arthur Knight, *Playboy*'s resident expert on "sex and the cinema," caught *Flaming Creatures* in Los Angeles on a bill with Stan Brakhage's work-in-progress *Dog Star Man* and, describing it for the readers of *The Saturday Review*, was suitably appalled: "A faggoty stag-reel, it comes as close to hardcore pornography as anything ever presented in a theater... Everything is shown in sickening detail, defiling at once both sex and cinema." [5]

[5] Arthur Knight, *The Saturday Review* (11/2/63).

EVERYTHING? AS THE FILMMAKER GREGORY MARKOPOULOS suggested in his impassioned account of the *Flaming Creatures* premiere (delivered at New York University in June 1964, a time when the movie itself was the subject of a criminal trial only a few subway stops away), *Flaming Creatures*'s original viewers were "projected into a state of cosmic or filmic shock."

Those images, scenes, and sequences that they had envisioned and had wished would appear in the commercial film that they attended were unexpectedly offered before their eyes.

[6] "Innocent Revels, *Film Culture* NO. 33 (SUMMER 1964) P.41.

Ken Kelman's account of the reception is quite different:

When the first show was over, a clique, a claque of six or so, back on the west side applauded, amid the numb and blind. Amid the tame, I halted, oppressed by their inertia, paused, vacillated, considered for two beats of silence or three, before I clapped solo and thus no doubt branded myself a clappy pervert, crap happy degenerate, slobbering sadist, or, even, perhaps Jack Smith.

"Smith Myth," *Film Culture* NO. 29 (SUMMER 1963) P.5.

"THE AUDIENCE BURST FORTH AND ROARED," MARKOPOULOS wrote, "while the walls of censorship began to crack." [6]

Flaming Creatures
frame enlargement
(JOEL MARKMAN, left;
SHEILA BICK, right)

SUCH WALLS WERE REAL. AT THE GRAMERCY ARTS, WHERE *Flaming Creatures* was shown twice in August to packed crowds ("At last! An evening of Baudelairean cinema" proclaimed the *Voice* ad), police harassment had become a regular feature of the show. Because the films exhibited were not submitted to the New York State Board of Regents for licensing, it was deemed illegal to charge admission for their exhibition. Mekas's counter-strategy was to present the movies free and solicit contributions for the Love and Kisses to Censors Film Society. When *Flaming Creatures* was shown it was advertised merely as "a film praised by Allen Ginsberg, Andy Warhol, Jean-Luc Godard, Diane Di Prima, Peter Beard, John Fles, Walter Gutman, Gregory Corso, Ron Rice, Storm De Hirsch, and everybody else." [7]

[7] *Midnight Movies*,
OP.CIT., P.59.

DRAWING EVER MORE ATTENTION TO *Flaming Creatures*, Mekas rented the midtown Tivoli Theater, a seedy venue known for sex exploitation films, to present Smith with *Film Culture*'s annual Independent Filmmaker Award. *Flaming Creatures* "has graced the anarchic liberation of new American cinema." Jack Smith

> has attained for the first time in motion pictures a high level of art which is absolutely lacking in decorum; and a treatment of sex which makes us aware of the restraint of all previous film-makers. [8]

[8] "Fifth Independent Film Award," *Film Culture*
NO. 29 (SUMMER 1963) P.I.

DECEMBER 2, MOMENTS BEFORE THE CEREMONIAL MIDNIGHT screening was to begin, the theater management buckled under the pressure from the city's Bureau of Licenses and canceled the show. Outraged, Mekas gave Smith his award outside, using the roofs of the cars parked along Eighth Avenue as his stage. Then, a few hundred New American Cinema partisans led by Barbara Rubin, one of the young firebrands of the Film-Makers' Cooperative, occupied the Tivoli until evacuated by the police. In a boxed statement printed in the next issue of *The Village Voice,* *Film Culture* spoke for all filmmakers: "We'll find places to show our work. We'll screen our movies in public places, on the highway billboards and in the streets, if necessary." [9]

9 "A Statement on *Flaming Creatures,*" *The Village Voice* (12/12/63).

Handbill, Jack Smith, 1963

LESS THAN A MONTH LATER, the *Flaming Creatures* crusade went international. Mekas had been invited to judge an experimental film festival in Knokke-le-Zout, Belgium. When *Flaming Creatures* was refused a screening, he resigned from the jury, threatened to withdraw the entries of other American filmmakers (including KENNETH ANGER, STAN BRAKHAGE, ROBERT BREER, and GREGORY MARKOPOULOS), and organized special showings in his hotel room. Among those present, perched on the bathtub or bed, were Jean-Luc Godard, Agnes Varda, and Roman Polanski. [10]

10 Leslie Trumbull, "Movie Journal," *The Village Voice* (1/9/64), P.13; *Sight and Sound* (SPRING 1964), P.89; "Knokke-le-Zout," *Film Quarterly* (SPRING 1964), P.14.

Flaming Creatures
frame enlargement
(JOEL MARKMAN)

WITH THE IRREPRESSIBLE BARBARA RUBIN AS HIS CONFEDERATE, Mekas chose New Year's Eve to commandeer the projection booth of the festival theater. Pretending to tie up the projectionist, filmmaker Jean-Marie Bouchet, and screening a print smuggled into the booth between the reels of Warhol's six-hour *Sleep*, Mekas provoked a disturbance that was widely reported in Europe. A small riot broke out, and as the Belgian Minister of Justice (and honorary head of the festival) arrived to quell it, Mekas projected the film on the minister's face until all power was cut off.

ULTIMATELY, THE JURY AWARDED *Flaming Creatures* A SPECIAL "damned" film prize. According to Mekas, most of the jurors thought they had seen a documentary. "A wild image of America we left in Knokke-le-Zout, I tell you," he reported in *The Village Voice*. "No wonder a State Department man was sitting next to our table wherever we went." [11]

[11] *Movie Journal,* OP.CIT., PP.III—I5.

Flaming Creatures MADE *Variety*'S FRONT PAGE AFTER KNOKKE-LE-ZOUT AND NOT FOR the last time. But if, as the show biz bible reported on January 15, "Belgians Balk N.Y. *Creatures*," New York itself was cleaning up for the 1964 World's Fair. Village coffee houses and Off-Off Broadway theaters were shuttered; Times Square tango palaces and taxi dance halls were closed; Lenny Bruce was arrested for obscenity at the Café Au Go Go. Unlicensed screenings of underground movies were hounded from venue to venue. On February 3, *Flaming Creatures* was shown with *Normal Love* rushes at the Gramercy Arts. Two weeks later, the theater was shut down.

THE NEXT SCREENINGS WERE AT THE NEW BOWERY THEATER at 4 St. Marks Place where, on February 20, Smith had projected *Normal Love* production slides to the accompaniment of a taped radio speech by Antonin Artaud. *Flaming Creatures* was shown, together with Andy Warhol's newsreel *Jack Smith Filming Normal Love*, on Monday, March 2, with an undercover policeman in the audience. The following night, two NYPD detectives broke up a near-capacity showing attended by some ninety spectators. "It was hot enough to burn up the screen," one cop would tell the press. [12]

12 Paul Meskil, "Police Chill 'Flaming' Movie," *New York World Telegram* (3/4/64).

THE POLICE IMPOUNDED BOTH FILMS, THE PROJECTOR, AND the screen, arresting the theater manager, Jacobs, and ticket-taker Florence Karpf. "The most articulate porn audience ever assembled were dressing down the cops," Jacobs recalled.

Poet Diane di Prima ducked out to phone Jonas. He rushed over and leaped in swinging the First Amendment. He insisted that if we were to be arrested, he be arrested as well, and forced information on them of his connection to the screening... At the stationhouse, Jonas was just as fiery... [It] was a bad scene, with movie-imitating killer cops, and I feared Jonas was going to bring it down on us. We were "fags" and "weirdos" (intellectuals) and "commies"... [13]

[13] Ken Jacobs, unpublished letter to *The Village Voice* (10/21/91); see also *Movie Journal*, OP.CIT., PP.129–30.

THE CAMPAIGN AGAINST FAGS, WEIRDOS, AND COMMIES WAS not restricted to New York. Saturday evening, March 7, Los Angeles police raided the Cinema theater and confiscated the print of Kenneth Anger's *Scorpio Rising*—"a purely homosexual thing," one member of the vice squad termed it. Theater manager Mike Getz was soon after arraigned for "exhibiting an obscene film." On the very same night in New York, Mekas was arrested once more—this time for showing Jean Genet's 1950 short *Un Chant d'Amour*, a poetic evocation of homosexual fantasy set in a French prison. [14]

[14] J. Hoberman, "License for License," *Banned in the U.S.A.: America and Film Censorship* (BERKELEY: PACIFIC FILM ARCHIVES, 1993), P.16.

THE *Chant d'Amour* SCREENING, AT THE WRITERS STAGE Theatre on East 4TH Street, was advertised as a benefit for the *Flaming Creatures* defense fund. Mekas's strategy was to link the suppression of *Flaming Creatures* to the suppression of a film, also suggesting graphic sexual acts and featuring male nudity, by a famous European artist ("push the prestigious Genet in their faces, pull in Sartre," Jacobs recalled). But, as Mekas reported from jail in *The Village Voice*: "The detectives who seized [*Un Chant d'Amour*] did not know who Genet was. When I told them that Genet was an internationally known artist, I was told it was my fantasy...

I was [also] told that they will make a statue of me in Washington Square; that they will make "a mashed potato" of me by the time they are through; that I was "dirtying America"; that I was fighting windmills. One of the detectives who arrested me told me, at the theatre, that he did not know why they were taking me to the station: I should be shot right there in front of the screen. [15]

[15] Jacobs, unpublished letter OP.CIT.; *Movie Journal*, OP.CIT., PP.129–30.

Flaming Creatures AND ***Scorpio Rising*** WERE BUSTED ONCE more at the New Bowery—on March 17—before the theater, which had been screening the movies free of charge, was padlocked. There were no more public showings as Mekas devoted his energies to the upcoming trial, his defense funded by Jerome Hill and abetted by a handful of academics, an assortment of beat poets, and the newly formed New York City League for Sexual Freedom (which demonstrated outside the D.A.'s office).

THE CASE, ***People of the State of New York vs. Kenneth Jacobs, Florence Karpf and Jonas Mekas***, was taken by the prominent civil rights lawyer Emile Zola Berman, who, according to newspaper accounts, at times thought he was representing the exhibitors of a film entitled ***Crimson Creatures***. Nevertheless, according to Judge David Trager, then a young lawyer working on the case, Berman (whose most notorious subsequent client would be Sirhan Sirhan, the assassin of Robert Kennedy) believed that ***New York vs. Jacobs*** had the potential to go to the United States Supreme Court. [16]

[16] David Trager, unpublished interview with J.H. (5/13/96).

DEFENDING *Flaming Creatures* IN THE APRIL 13 ISSUE OF *The Nation*, Susan Sontag scored "the indifference, the squeamishness, the downright hostility to the film evinced by almost everyone in the mature intellectual and artistic community." Although this squeamishness extended to *The Nation* (Sontag later recalled that the editor who assigned her the piece was fired as a result) and beyond (on April 7, the Modern Museum in Stockholm cancelled a New American Cinema series that might have featured *Flaming Creatures*), "mature" support may not have mattered. The three-judge Criminal Court panel, which included former New York City mayor Vincent Impellitteri, refused to allow expert testimony, with the single exception of Sontag's, on either *Flaming Creatures*'s artistic merit or its alleged pornography. [17]

FILM HISTORIAN Herman Weinberg, producer Lewis Allen, poet Allen Ginsburg, and filmmakers Shirley Clarke and Willard Van Dyke took the stand in vain; the prosecution case rested entirely on treating the judges to a screening. "Two of them munching cigars, watched impassively as the movie was shown in chambers," one daily reported. [18]

[17] Stephanie Gervis Harrington, "Pornography is Undefined at Film-Critic Mekas' Trial," *The Village Voice* (6/18/64), P.9.

[18] Paul Hoffman, "A Movie Show—in Criminal Court," *New York Post* (6/3/64), P.16.

Smith's recollections of the *Flaming Creatures* affair may be found in his 1978 interview with Sylvere Lotringer. *Flaming Creatures* was confiscated, Smith explains, because "Mekas was into having something in court at that time, very fashionable, a lot of publicity..."

He would give screenings of *Creatures* and making [sic] speeches, defying the police to bust the film. Which they did. And then there was the trial... I walked into the courtroom and my lawyer said "Go out of the courtroom," and I said "Why?"—"Because the judge is upset by too many men with beards." I was ordered to leave by that marshmallow lawyer that Uncle Mekas had. So I couldn't even see the trial.

"Uncle Fishook and the Sacred Baby Poo-Poo of Art," *Wait for Me at the Bottom of the Pool: The Writings of Jack Smith*, ed. J. Hoberman and Edward Leffingwell (LONDON: SERPENT'S TAIL/ HIGH RISK BOOKS, 1997), PP.107–8.

As a defendant, Ken Jacobs has a somewhat different memory of the trial. He and Flo Karpf were the jerks, jerked around for months on end from hearing to hearing, never speaking in court, passed up by reporters, even snubbed by our own counsel the self-promoting Emile Zola Berman... Only his fine but intimidated assistant David Traeger [sic] would speak with us. Berman would actually lead Jonas away from us to confer, the grown-ups, in privacy.

Jack bothered just once to observe a court session. He left without a word but clearly disdainful, as if we were fools for involving ourselves in this, like we had a choice. And one time some of us, defendants and supporters, went off to Mott Street for lunch where whenever I spoke Susan Sontag acted as if the furniture had the effrontery to interrupt her.

Jacobs, unpublished letter OP.CIT.

45

ON JUNE 12, JACOBS AND MEKAS WERE CONVICTED AND sentenced to sixty days in the New York City workhouse. The trial was followed, four days later, and to some extent upstaged by *People of the State of New York vs. Lenny Bruce*, which ran for months in the same Criminal Courts Building and resulted in Bruce's conviction for giving an "indecent performance." Jacobs's and Mekas's sentences were suspended, as was Karpf's, but the court ruling has never been reversed. (Technically, *Flaming Creatures* remains obscene, at least in the boroughs of Manhattan and the Bronx, to this day.)

As *New York vs. Jacobs* WORKED ITS WAY THROUGH THE courts, *Flaming Creatures* rocked the film societies of the nation's universities. On April 1, 1965 (a week after the first teach-in against the war in Vietnam was held at the University of Michigan in Ann Arbor), Albuquerque police raided an off-campus screening arranged by University of New Mexico students, who claimed that the film's star was a UNM graduate, and confiscated the print. [19]

ANOTHER SCREENING—ORGANIZED BY THE LOCAL CHAPTER of Students for a Democratic Society (by then the largest organization of campus radicals in America) a month after the *Flaming Creatures* case reached the United States Supreme Court—was broken up on November 9, 1966, at the University of Texas in Austin. SDS, which recognized a hot issue when it saw one, was also involved in an incident at the University of Michigan, two months later. By then, much to the displeasure of *The New York Times* senior movie critic Bosley Crowther, the underground had surfaced: Andy Warhol's *Chelsea Girls* was playing at a midtown Manhattan movie house. On January 5, 1967 the *Times* announced that "Adult Themes Head for Screen." [20]

[19] "Albuquerque Axes Avant-Garde Film About 'Third Sex,'" *Variety* (4/7/65), P.1.

[20] "Film Showing Cancelled After Police Enter 'Y,'" *The Daily Texan* (11/10/66), P.1. Bosley Crowther, "The Underground Overflows," *The New York Times* (12/11/66).

46

THE EVENING OF JANUARY 18, ACTING ON A PROFESSOR'S complaint, an Ann Arbor police officer halted the *Flaming Creatures* screening at the Architecture School auditorium just as the Rape-Earthquake-Orgy sequence commenced, fifteen minutes and thirty seconds into the movie. A group of irate students initially blocked the officer's exit from the booth. Later, a hundred or so marched downtown to stage a four-hour sit-in at the station house demanding the film's return. Three student members of the Cinema Guild and their faculty advisor were arraigned on charges of showing an obscene motion picture. [21]

THE SUBSEQUENT HEARINGS, LAWSUITS, AND TRIAL PREOCCUPIED Ann Arbor for the remainder of the year when, unmoved by history professor Robert Sklar's defense testimony, a municipal judge ruled *Flaming Creatures* "a smutty purveyance of filth [that] borders on the razor's edge of hard-core pornography." By that time, the *Flaming Creatures* appeal had been mooted by five of the nine justices of the United States Supreme Court. The four dissenting justices were split: Chief Justice Warren and Justice Brennan voted to affirm the judgment of the lower court while Justices Fortas and Douglas voted to reverse the judgment. [22]

THIS FOOTNOTE BECAME A FOOTBALL WHEN, IN THE SUMMER OF 1968, lame duck president Lyndon Johnson nominated Fortas for chief justice. In the Fortas nomination, Senate conservatives found a way to attack the entire Warren court. Their weapon would be Fortas's liberal rulings on pornography. The print of *Flaming Creatures* confiscated in Ann Arbor was flown to Washington, DC, at the behest of Senator Strom Thurmond, the ranking Republican on the Senate Judiciary Committee. The senator "already has some experience as a film critic," *Variety* noted. "He recently railed against *The New York Times* for criticizing *The Green Berets*." [23]

[21] "Underground Film is Seized at U. of Michigan Showing," *The New York Times* (1/20/67); "Transvestite *Flaming Creatures* Pic Raided," *Variety* (1/25/67).

[22] "Municipal Judge Says *Flaming Creatures* Obscene," *The Ann Arbor News* (9/1/67) p.15. Bruce Allen Murphy, *Fortas: The Rise and Fall of a Supreme Court Judge* (NEW YORK: WILLIAM MORROW, 1988), p.448.

On January 15, 1968, another *Flaming Creatures* print was impounded by New York District Attorney Robert Morgenthau on its return to the Film-Makers' Cooperative after a booking in Vancouver. At the same time, the movie continued to be screened. Ads clipped from Los Angeles newspapers in late February 1969 announce *Flaming Creatures* showing in an "approved edited version" at the Park theatre. In May, the movie was screened openly at Cinematheque, then returned to the Park for a week in mid-July. In the interim, the Warhol Factory previewed their bluntly titled *Fuck* (which would be busted the following month as *Blue Movie*) and transvestites battled New York cops over the closing of the Stonewall bar in Greenwich Village.

[23] "Try to Put Torch to Fortas Nomination by Showing *Flaming Creatures* in D.C.," *Variety* (7/31/68), p.62.

IN LATE JULY, THURMOND ORGANIZED A "FORTAS FILM Festival" in Room 2228 of the Senate office building. A fourteen-minute filmed striptease, two other skin flicks, and *Flaming Creatures* were projected on the wood-paneled wall. Members of Congress were invited, as was the press, and Thurmond, who claimed that he had "shocked Washington's hardened press corps," thoughtfully furnished glossy frame-enlargements from the movie. [24]

The anti-Fortas forces announced plans to send prints of *Flaming Creatures* to women's groups and civic clubs in hopes of triggering further outrage. Before the Fortas nomination collapsed in September, there was talk of showing the film on the Senate floor. Although that last screening never came to pass, *Flaming Creatures* is likely the only American avant-garde movie ever described in *The Congressional Record*. This "home made film," the *Record* reads, "has gained a notorious reputation for its homosexual content.

> [It] presents five unrelated, badly filmed sequences, which are studded with sexual symbolisms... a mass rape scene involving two females and many males, which lasts for seven minutes, showing the female pubic area, the male penis, males massaging the female vagina and breasts, cunnilingus, masturbation of the male organ, and other sexual symbolisms... lesbian activity between two women... homosexual acts between a man dressed as a female, who emerges from a casket, and other males, including masturbation of the visible male organ... homosexuals dancing together and other disconnected erotic activity, such as massaging the female breasts and group sexual activity. [25]

[24] John Corry, "Washington Report: Strom's Dirty Movies," *Harper's* (DECEMBER 1968), PP.30–40.

[25] *Congressional Record—House* (9/4/68) P.25562.

48

Flaming Creatures
frame enlargement
(PIERO HELICZER, left;
MARIO MONTEZ, right)

THIS EARNEST TESTIMONY, AS HOPELESS AS IT IS GRAPHIC, was supplied by the founder of Citizens for Decent Literature, Cincinnati lawyer Charles Keating (convicted, twenty-five summers later, of seventy-three counts of fraud, racketeering, and conspiracy in defrauding Lincoln Savings and Loan Association and its investors). More suggestive was the account of *Flaming Creatures* an anonymous senator offered a *Newsweek* correspondent: "That movie was so sick," the senator explained, "I couldn't even get aroused." Thus, the movie's failure as pornography was something worse than pornography itself. [26]

26 Samuel Shaffer, *On and Off the Floor: Thirty Years as a Correspondent on Capitol Hill* (NEW YORK: NEWSWEEK BOOKS, 1980), P.92. Strom Thurmond aside, the senators known to have screened *Flaming Creatures* in Room 2228 on July 29, 1968, were James O. Eastland (Dem-Miss.), Russell B. Long (Dem-La.), John McClellan (Dem-Ark.), Gale McGee (Dem-Wyo.), and Jack Miller (Rep-Iowa). "Griffin Says 40 Ready to Block Vote on Fortas," *Washington Post* (7/29/68), P.A6.

Carel Rowe noted a similar response when he showed *Flaming Creatures* in spring 1972 as part of the Lurid Film Festival at Northwestern University. The audience laughed raucously for the first third and "then, suddenly, the crowd grew ugly," *The Baudelairean Cinema: A Trend within the American Avant-Garde* (ANN ARBOR, MI: UMI RESEARCH PRESS, 1982), P.XI.

WHILE *Flaming Creatures* WAS SCARCELY THE ONLY EXPLICIT movie produced by the early '60s underground, it triggered a rage that far exceeded the hostility directed at such other candidates for martyrdom as Stan Brakhage's *Window Water Baby Moving*, Carolee Schneeman's *Fuses*, or Barbara Rubin's *Christmas on Earth*. These movies were "merely" explicit—or, in the case of Jean Genet's venerable *Un Chant d'Amour* and Kenneth Anger's *Scorpio Rising* (two other movies that were prosecuted, albeit less forcefully), blatantly homoerotic. The behavior in *Flaming Creatures* is something else—extravagantly queer to be sure but even queerer than that.

THOSE RUDELY BRANDISHED DICKS, NEITHER WHOLLY ERECT nor entirely flaccid, are only penises. As funny as it is poignant, *Flaming Creatures* is guilty of a criminal disrespect more serious than burning the flag. In so casually representing the male organ, it desecrates the underlying symbol of all power structures—including the U.S. Senate.

DURING THE SUMMER OF 1962, THE PAINTER AND photographer Norman Solomon accompanied his friend Ray Johnson to the roof of the Windsor Theater and the set of *Flaming Creatures*. The one, only partially extant, roll of Kodachrome color slides and two rolls of black-and-white TriX film that Solomon shot are the only known documentation of the film's production. Evidently, the scene shot that day was a retake of the rape-orgy. In addition to Jack Smith, the identifiable participants are Sheila Bick, whom Solomon knew as Sheli Rappaport, Joel Markman, Arnold Rockwood, Mark Schleifer, and, assisting Smith, Billy Linich (later BILLY NAME). Solomon, who also remembered Henry Proach and Jerry Raphael as present, had no official connection with the movie: "I was 'merely there,' making photographs for the making of photographs." The pictures, selected from three separate rolls, are presented here in the order in which they were taken, using the original numbering.

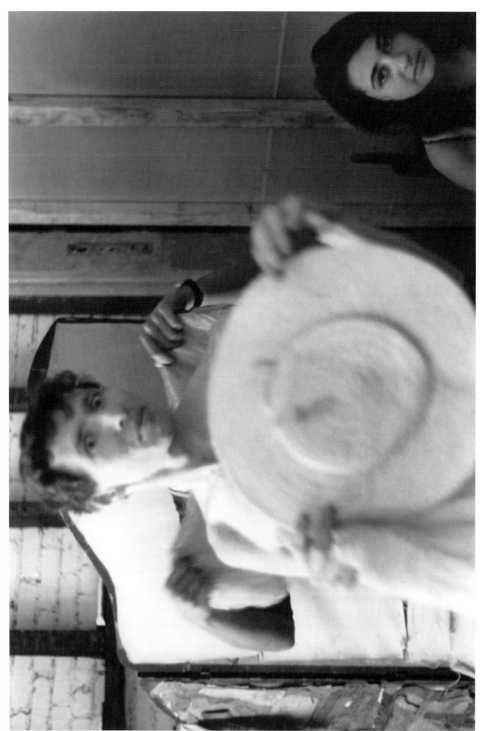

ROLL
1-23

ROLL
1-31

ROLL

11-2

ROLL

11-4

ROLL

11-8

ROLL
11-9

ROLL
11-10

ROLL
11–15

SLIDE
2

SLIDE

19

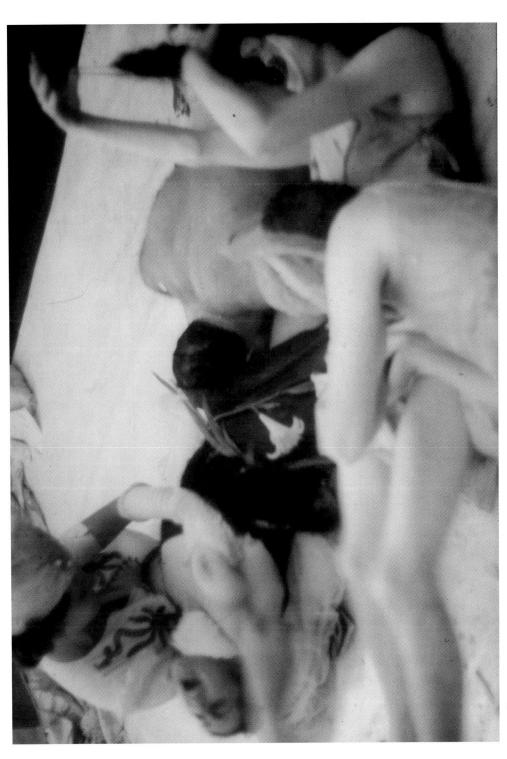

The Other Films

Untitled color print,
Jack Smith, circa 1959.
(BOB FLEISCHNER, center;
JERRY SIMS, right)

Untitled color print
Scotch Tape site,
Jack Smith, circa 1959.
(JERRY SIMS, left;
KEN JACOBS, right)

Scotch Tape

JACK SMITH, 1959–62, 3 MINS. COLOR.

WITH: Jerry Sims, Ken Jacobs, and Reese Haire (UNCREDITED).

MUSIC (UNCREDITED): *Carinhoso* (PETER DUCHIN).

RECORDING: Tony Conrad (UNCREDITED).

"*A* MASTER SENSE OF SPIRITUAL NOTHINGNESS... the most recent explosion of a major creative force in cinema has in this film filled a New Jersey [sic] junkyard with life and movement and spiritual weightlessness." — *Film-Makers' Cooperative Catalogue* NO. 4 (1967)

Scotch Tape, JACK SMITH's first released movie, is an apparently unedited 100-foot roll of Kodachrome II shot in 1959, using Ken Jacobs's Bell & Howell at one of Jacobs's *Star Spangled to Death* locations—the rubble-strewn site of the future Lincoln Center on Manhattan's West Side. [1]

"THAT DAY," P. ADAMS SITNEY writes, "Jacobs had assembled his cast in a destroyed building...

Rusted cables in great tangles and broken slabs of concrete were all about. Smith borrowed the camera and filmed a dance of people exuberantly hopping around and under the cables. The area of wreckage was so extensive that he could film his dancers either from a few feet away or from hundreds of feet above them. Only by the size of the human figure is the scale of the shot perceptible... [2]

[1] Ken Jacobs, unpublished letter to *The Village Voice* (10/21/91); Ken Jacobs, unpublished interview with J.H. (3/11/96).

Following *Scotch Tape*'s uncredited blurb in the *Film-Makers' Cooperative Catalogue*, Sheldon Renan's *An Introduction to the American Underground Film* mistakenly places the *Scotch Tape* location in New Jersey, as does John Fles's note in *Film Culture* NO. 34. In addition to *Scotch Tape*, Smith made a number of color tableau vivants (or, as he called them, plastiques) on the Lincoln Center site.

[2] *Visionary Film: The American Avant-Garde 1943–1978*, second edition (NEW YORK: OXFORD UNIVERSITY PRESS, 1979), P.339.

3 IBID., PP.339–40.

4 *Queer Theatre*
(FRANKFURT AM MAIN:
SUHRKAMP VERLAG, 1978),
p.24. Brecht believes that
the shot of the "blatantly
de-functionalised flower"
indicates that *Scotch Tape*
was, in fact, edited. This
seems unlikely although the
truth cannot be readily
ascertained as the camera
original has been lost.

In the longest shots [Smith] framed his group of actors in a corner of the cluttered image; then he positioned them under a covering slab of concrete so that in the brief duration of the shot the viewer must seek out the dancers in the visual field. In the closer shots he makes use of a green artificial flower under which they dance or which some of them hold in their teeth while jumping about. Once, the flower rests statically in focus while the blurred bodies vibrate in the background. [3]

Untitled color print
Jerry Sims at home,
Jack Smith, circa 1959.

DESPITE ITS BREVITY, *Scotch Tape* anticipates the epic quality of Smith's subsequent films and theater pieces. The alternation of long shots and close-ups suggest considerable elapsed time between each set-up.

TO JUDGE FROM THE hyperactive quality of these "cavortings," which Stefan Brecht describes as "partly the lady-like posturing gestures of inverts, partly jungle gym gamboling in some game of Tarzan," Smith may have effectively undercranked Jacobs's spring-wound camera. [4]

Untitled color print
Scotch Tape site,
Jack Smith, circa 1959.
(JERRY SIMS, standing
and KEN JACOBS.)

JACOBS, WHO APPEARS IN THE film, frantically dancing and mugging along with another *Star Spangled to Death* performer, Jerry Sims, proposed that Smith call his film *Reveling in the Dumps* and even drew titles. Instead, Smith chose to name his movie after the dirty piece of stickum that had wedged itself inside the camera gate and was consequently printed throughout in the upper right corner of the frame. [5]

FOR A THREE-MINUTE FILM, *Scotch Tape* carries considerable conceptual weight. The title anticipates Andy Warhol's go-with-the-flow acceptance of cinematic "mistakes," even as it draws the viewer's attention to the perceptual tension between the film's actual surface and its represented depth. That Smith's edited-in-camera montage juxtaposes long shots with extreme close-ups and involves radical shifts in focal length only serves to emphasize the tape's presence. "Its fixed position," as Sitney observes, "offers a formal counterbalance to the play of scales upon which the shot changes are based." [6]

Scotch Tape's AUDIO ACCOMpaniment was created, some three years later, by Tony Conrad, who, acting on Smith's instructions, cut Peter Duchin's rumba *Carinhoso* to match the footage. Watching the resultant sync event, Conrad later recalled, had a decisive effect on his own life, even inspiring him to become a filmmaker.

[5] Jacobs interview, OP. CIT.

Sitney reports that "since Jacobs seldom had enough money to develop his rushes from *Star Spangled to Death*, he had shot several rolls of film before he realized the tape had gotten caught in the camera," *Visionary Film*, OP. CIT., P.340.

Sitney interviewed Smith on the making of *Scotch Tape* in 1963 in order to help the filmmaker apply for a Ford Foundation grant. "What I wrote was a pale academic version of the hilarious and often brilliant responses [Smith] gave to my prodding," he later recalled.

> For instance, when I asked him how he got started as a film-maker, he intoned something a little like this: "I... I... I... I wanted delirium...uhhh, the tweeky effluvium of my photographs...But there was a little piece of scotch tape in Nutsy's (Ken Jacobs') camera. I... I... I loathe those pasty imperfections, but I... the film was ruined, disaster, the tape didn't even move... I mean the rhythm: it was strange, even better than the Lotus dance... uhhhh, that's the advantage for the flaming artist, I mean it's not the idea... futurism... You know, call the film *Scotch Tape*... I just put a soundtrack on it."

P. Adams Sitney, "Writing Jack Smith's Ford Foundation Application," *Film Culture* NO. 78 (SUMMER 1994), P.14.

[6] *Visionary Film*, OP.CIT., P.340.

7 Tony Conrad in David Reisman, "In the Grip of the Lobster: Jack Smith Remembered," *Millennium Film Journal* NO. 23/24 (WINTER 1990–91), PP.64–65; unpublished Tony Conrad interview with J.H. (5/10/96).

For an account of the Charles Theater and its importance as a venue for underground films, see J. Hoberman and Jonathan Rosenbaum, *Midnight Movies* (NEW YORK: HARPER & ROW, 1983), PP.40–46. For Smith's recollections of the Charles, see "Taboo of Jingola," *Wait for Me at the Bottom of the Pool: The Writings of Jack Smith*, ed. J. Hoberman and Edward Leffingwell (LONDON: SERPENT'S TAIL, 1997), PP.102–5.

All of a sudden, a commitment emerged, a kind of special pleasure that reached out and grabbed the whole scene in a way that was inhabited by a very very special comic presence. And it was on the way to ecstasy, and in fact, it was ecstasy. And at that point, I was won over to be a filmmaker; it was such an extraordinary thing to see, what happened to sound in the presence of a moving image.

CONRAD PLACES THIS SCREENING at the Charles Theater, which would date it to the summer of 1962. [7]

ON FEBRUARY 11, 1963, *Scotch Tape* was programmed by Jonas Mekas, along with Jacobs's *Little Stabs at Happiness*, the Jacobs-Fleischer Smith portrait *Blonde Cobra*, Ron Rice's *Senseless*, and films by Bhob Stewart and Ray Wisniewski, at the Bleecker Street Cinema under the rubric "Newest Absurd and Zen Poetry." Smith's records indicate a check for the composite *Scotch Tape* print, provided by Mekas and dated a week before the *Flaming Creatures* premiere, April 22, 1963. John Fles's brief appreciation, published in *Film Culture* NO. 34, is based on seeing *Scotch Tape* in Los Angeles during the summer of 1963.

Flaming Creatures ASIDE, *Scotch Tape* would be Smith's only completed film—it was placed in distribution with the Film-Makers' Cooperative in 1962 and subsequently included in Anthology Film Archives's Essential Cinema.

Overstimulated

1959–63, 6 MINS. B&W. SILENT

WITH: Jerry Sims and Bob Fleischner.

SHOT IN BLACK AND WHITE IN SMITH'S LOWER EAST SIDE apartment (the location for *Blonde Cobra*), *Overstimulated* features Bob Fleischner and Jerry Sims—a sometime Smith model, also prominent in Ken Jacobs's *Star Spangled to Death*—wearing long, filmy dresses and jumping up and down in front of a flickering television set. The camera work is scarcely less frantic; made after *Scotch Tape*, the film likely dates from late 1959, before Smith and Fleischner had their falling out. Smith's records show that Jonas Mekas wrote a check, dated August 7, 1963, to cover the cost of printing *Overstimulated*. The film may have been briefly distributed by the Film-Makers' Cooperative. Smith withdrew the negative, along with *Flaming Creatures* two years later. Two years after that it was incorporated in the program *Horror and Fantasy at Midnight* which subsequently evolved into *No President*.

Handbill, Jack Smith, November 1967.

Paper Dolls

RICHARD PRESTON, 1962, 4½ MINS. COLOR.

STILLS BY Jack Smith and Girlie Mags.
MUSIC: Dick Andrews (JAPANESE FLUTE).

> *An experiment with the hand-held photograph and a little animation... Based on the Thomas Dekkar stanza: "Beauty is but a flower/which wrinkles will devour/ death fall from the air/dust hath closed Helen's eye/I am sick, I must die/Lord have mercy on us."* —R.P.

*B*EST KNOWN FOR HIS SATIRICAL CUT-AND-PASTE COLLAGE-animations, the Australian filmmaker photographer Richard Preston was an active participant in the New York underground from the late 1950s through the late 1960s. Preston's early films incorporated printed material ranging from Jules Feiffer cartoons and pulp magazine illustrations to ads for the Hedy Lamarr movie *Ecstasy*.

From *The Beautiful Book*,
Jack Smith, circa 1962.
(MARIAN ZAZEELA, center;
JOEL MARKMAN, right.)

SOMETIME AFTER SMITH "USED and wrecked" Preston's Brooklyn darkroom during the spring of 1961, Preston printed a number of Smith's black-and-white negatives—many of them culled from the 1961–62 shooting sessions that produced *The Beautiful Book*. These were filmed, interspersed with photographs of nude pin-ups cut out from men's magazines.

In the context of 1962, Smith's photographs were shocking—the young Tony Conrad, for one, initially experienced them as pornographic. Nevertheless (and whether intentional on Preston's part or not), the tension created in *Paper Dolls* between Smith's posings and the mildly prurient T&A erotica of the day is considerable—and almost interesting.

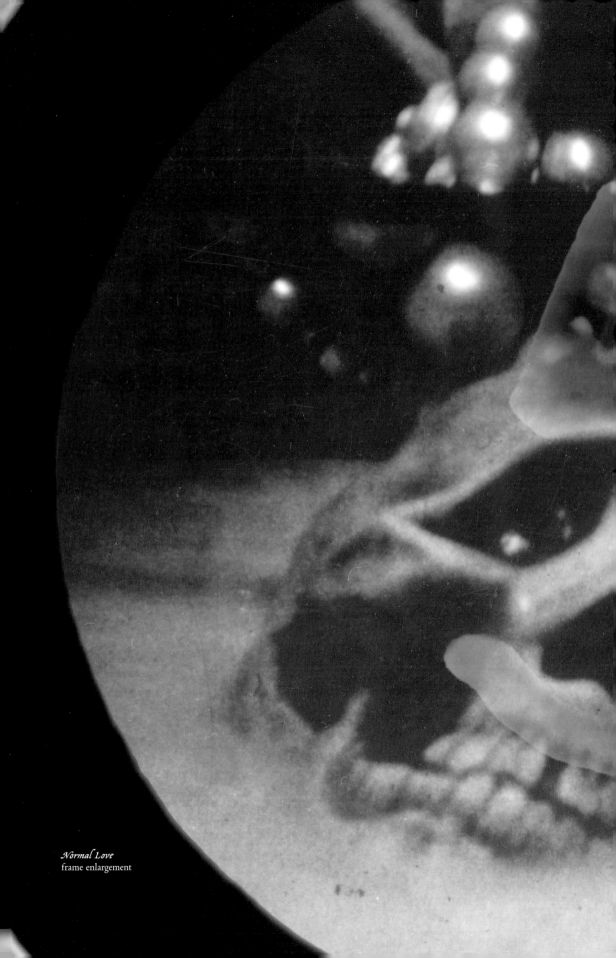

Normal Love
frame enlargement

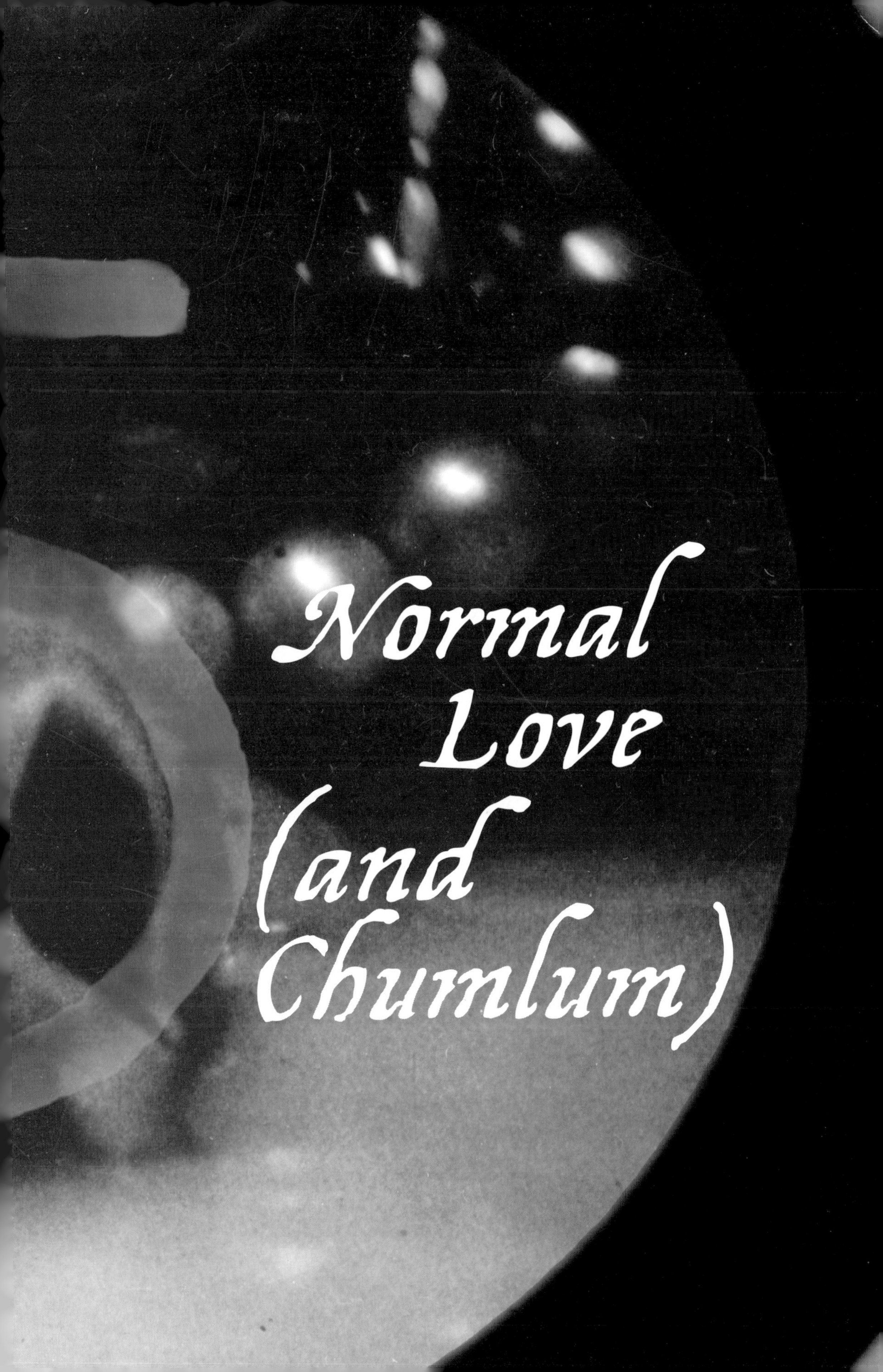

Normal
Love
(and
Chumlum)

Normal Love frame enlargement (MARIO MONTEZ)

Normal Love (The Yellow Sequence), production still (DAVID SACHS, left; FRANCIS FRANCINE)

Normal Love

JACK SMITH, 1963–64, 105 MINS. COLOR.

CAST: Mario Montez (MERMAID); Diana Baccus (THE GIRL); David Sachs (MONGOLIAN CHILD); Angus MacLise (THE GREEN MUMMY); Beverly Grant (COBRA WOMAN); Naomi Levine (BLACK SPIDER); Francis Francine (PINK FAIRY; THE CAKE GIRL); Tony Conrad (THE MUMMY); Tiny Tim (GILDED HAG); Sheila Bick (COBRA LADY); Eliot Cuker (WEREWOLF); John Vaccaro (WHITE BAT); Joan Adler (CHORUS CUTIE); Diane Di Prima (PREGNANT CUTIE); Arnold Rockwood (UNCLE PASTY); Teddy Howard (WATERMELON MAN); Johnny Foster (POOL CREATURE). [1]

The Yellow Sequence

(*Normal Love* ADDENDUM)

JACK SMITH, 1963, 20 MINS. COLOR.

WITH: Francis Francine, Tiny Tim, and David Sachs.

> *The whole of western culture exudes the distinctive aroma*
> *of slowing frying mermaid filleted.*
> —JACK SMITH TO JONAS MEKAS, SUMMER 1963.

COMPLAINING, EVEN BEFORE THE *Flaming Creatures* bust of March 1964, about the "sickeningly pasty reception" his film had received, Jack Smith wrote in his journal that he "was not likely to make another movie that the people of [his] own city could not see." The statement proved prophetic. Smith would never complete another film—at least in conventional terms. [2]

[1] Uncredited participants include Stanley Alboum, Joel Markman, Alan Marlowe, Patty Oldenburg, and Andy Warhol. *Normal Love*'s opening titles, created by Alboum, also give credit for a never-assembled musical track by Tony Conrad, Angus MacLise, and Robert Adler.

[2] "The Astrology of a Movie Scorpio," *Wait for Me at the Bottom of the Pool: The Writings of Jack Smith*, ed. J. Hoberman and Edward Leffingwell (LONDON: SERPENT'S TAIL, 1997), P.55.

[3] IBID.

In an undated interview with Jonas Mekas, most likely made in mid August 1963, Smith elaborated on his technique.

Mother Cinema is a jealous mistress. Often I realize half-way through a take that I've forgotten to direct a creature, or the creatures, in the shot. At the beginning of the shot they think they know what the shot is about, what we're doing, but then after a while they sort of exhaust some little cutie-pie thing that they'd thought of and then realize that the take is in the middle; so they look towards the camera usually, puzzled, sort of a chipmunk concentration, sort of looking, shrugging in a way that will be so much against the atmosphere of what's happening about them that only I, only the director, looking through the viewfinder will know, will catch this, and tell them what to do.

[4] "The Great Pasty Triumph," *Film Culture* NO. 29 (SUMMER 1963) P.6.

Mekas calls his brief appreciation after *Normal Love*'s working title—one Smith would several times recycle. "The Great Pasty Triumph" was also the rubric for his last one-person photography show, at the Erewhon Gallery, 41 East 1ST Street, in January 1965. The exhibition included a number of pre-1962 color images

The most extensive and atmospheric account of the *Normal Love* shoot is Joan Adler's *On Location*, published as the first chapter in Stephen Dwoskin, *Film Is: The International Free Cinema* (WOODSTOCK NY: THE OVERLOOK PRESS, 1975), PP.11–22.

FIRST, HOWEVER, AS BACKED by Jonas Mekas (himself funded by the filmmaker-philanthropist JEROME HILL), Smith embarked on a "commercial" follow-up to *Flaming Creatures*: "I spent my summer out in the country shooting a lovely, pasty, pink and green color movie that is going to be the definitive pasty expression. All the characters wear pink evening gowns and smirk and stare into the camera." [3]

The Great Pasty Triumph, known briefly as *The Pink and Green Horrors* and eventually retitled *Normal Love*, was very much a film of its

(many of which anticipate *Normal Love* in posing elaborately costumed creatures in natural settings) affixed to three-inch white wooden cubes. The small ad in *The Village Voice* (2/4/65) promised that "Free Ritz Crackers With Lobster Flavored Wallpaper Dip Will Be Served."

season. With the exception of several scenes staged around the Moon Pool, a candle-lit, incense-shrouded, mirror-strewn altar to Maria Montez, which Smith had assembled in the midst of an East Village apartment, it was strictly back to nature—shot variously in rural New Jersey, on Fire Island, in Queens, and at Old Lyme, Connecticut. Smith uses leaves, branches, smoke, sparklers, confetti, and all manner of gauze to clutter up the foreground and create compositions where performers blend into the decor. The dominant colors are pink and green—fittingly, one scene is a ceremonial watermelon feast. "Rubens. Arabian Nights. Chinese Masters. Monet... It is a dream that Jack must have carried in himself since his childhood, this pink-yellow Chinese-Arabic dream," Jonas Mekas rhapsodized after seeing the first rushes. [4]

IN FACT, *Normal Love* suggests a pastoral, pastel-colored conflation of *Frankenstein Meets the Wolf Man*, *The Lady and the Monster*, *I Walked with a Zombie*, *The Mummy's Hand*, and *The Spider Woman*. Even more than *Flaming Creatures*, its successor drew upon the "secret-flix" of Smith's boyhood—specifically those Universal wartime horror-movies whose stars (BELA LUGOSI and GALE SONDERGAARD) he particularly admired and would re-imagine. There is even a spot for Deanna Durbin, the actress *The New York Times* called "the Watteau shepherdess of Universal Pictures," but, for Smith's fellow Montez-enthusiast Ronald Tavel, that which Mekas saw as a "Chinese-Arabic dream" was a work that obviously drew "its look, its feel, its colors, images, and backyard fairy moth sheen directly from *White Savage*." [5]

THE NOTES THAT SMITH prepared for Tony Conrad's never-completed soundtrack refer to six distinct sequences The opening Red Scene, an interior with the Mermaid and the Black Spider, precedes the title and credits. These are followed by the Watteau-like Swing Scene, in which The Girl (DIANA BACCUS) is pursued through a leafy glade, and then pushed in a swing by the Watermelon Man. The lighting of sparklers creates a strategic fade to the Swamp Sequence. Here, The Girl squints in the sun as she's stalked through a verdant marsh by Uncle Pasty, the beefy, cunnilingual rapist from *Flaming Creatures*. In addition to the mask worn in the earlier film, Pasty sports a set of trick-store fangs that come loose when The Girl deflects his attentions—and causes him to fall out of character—with a custard-pie in the kisser. [6]

[5] "Maria Montez: Anima of an Antediluvian World," *Jack Smith, Flaming Creature— His Amazing Life and Times*, ed. Edward Leffingwell (LONDON: SERPENT'S TAIL/PS 1 MUSEUM, 1997), p.96. Smith's own account of his secret-flix is found in "Perfect Filmic Appositeness," *Wait for Me*, OP.CIT., PP.25–35. Smith's evaluation of then-current trash movies anticipates our own situation: "Fantasies now feature weight lifters who think now how lucky and clever they were to get into the movies & the fabulous pay" P.28.

[6] A selection of Smith's *Normal Love* journal notes appear in *Wait for Me*, OP.CIT., PP.45–50. (The piece titled *Normal Love*, however, shares only its title with the movie.)

FILM CULTURE

NO. 29 SUMMER 1963 $1.00

AMERICA'S INDEPENDENT MOTION PICTURE MAGAZINE

SPECIAL ISSUE: AMERICAN DIRECTORS, PART 2

Film Culture cover, 1963

7 The Werewolf is played by Elliot Cuker (or Cukor). Whether or not this Elliot Cuker grew up to be the luxury car dealer and "former actor" frequently reported in the New York tabloids of the late 1990s as a friend of the city's mayor Rudolph Guiliani is a subject for further research.

8 Robert Adler's uncredited photograph of Smith preparing to filmed the Cake Scene graces the cover of *Film Culture*'s summer 1963 issue. Andy Warhol shot a one-roll 16mm "newsreel" of the sequence, confiscated by the New York City Police Department in March 1964 and presumably lost.

Normal Love DOESN'T HAVE *Flaming Creatures*'s stone-age quality. Despite the Swamp Sequence's regressive trajectory —it ends with a handsome, if slime-covered, druggy-looking Werewolf rising from the primeval muck to assault the increasingly disheveled Mermaid, the equally dazed camera spinning overhead, and offer her a Coke—it's less an orgy than a reverie. That the action is punctuated with shots of the Mermaid's milk bath reinforces the suggestion in Smith's papers that much of the movie might be taking place in her "inner psychotic world." 7

THE SWAMP SEQUENCE IS followed by the blue scene in which comatose creatures in pink gowns lounge, as if after the ball, around the faux classical sculptures that guard the imposing swimming pool of the extravagantly rococo Belvedere Guest House built in the style of a Venetian palace by John Eberhardt in Cherry Grove, Fire Island. This languorous sequence is succeeded by leafy darkness of the lengthy Green Scene, featuring the Mummy and the Cobra Woman with her boa constrictor, then the bucolic Party Scene—shot in a cow pasture and thus extending the theme of milk from the Mermaid's bath to the colored drinks the creatures quaff—and the famous Cake Scene. 8

THIS OPEN-AIR TRIBUTE TO Busby Berkeley shifts gears only slightly when the Pink Faery (FRANCIS FRANCINE) emerges from the cake and the emerald-green Mummy (TONY CONRAD, sewn into his costume) lurches out to abduct one cutie before being himself mowed down by the skinny, demented-looking, machine-gun-toting Mongolian Child. David Sachs, the young political activist who played the role, remembers that his plastic machine gun broke early in the scene, the result of "slamming it into the ground in my mongoloid frenzy."

OVER THE AUGUST 11–12 weekend, while *Flaming Creatures* and *Scotch Tape* played the Gramercy, Smith took his *Normal Love* cast on location at the Connecticut estate of Stable gallery-owner Eleanor Ward. Out in the meadow, Smith topped a giant pink-and-white layer cake (constructed from Claes Oldenburg's macquette) with a score of writhing, half-naked male and female "chorus cuties," including a barely discernible Andy Warhol dancing behind a very pregnant Diane di Prima. "We were shimmying like crazy all over that cake," di Prima recalled, "We did about 80,000 takes [and] each time we did a take I fell off the cake." [9]

It was essentially in two pieces, hanging by a thread. This accounts for the odd way I held it thereafter. I was inwardly quite upset. Jack, I think, was unfazed. Like my falling on top of the cake, or the mermaid losing her wig in the slime, it was another opportunity. The film's development was open to possibility, fluid, like a marihuana-reverie, or real life. [10]

[9] Diane di Prima, unpublished interview with J.H. (4/30/96).

[10] David Sachs, e-mail to J.H. (9/29/2000).

SMITH'S CHRONOLOGY ENDS with the cake scene although *Normal Love* includes one further scene, referred to in Smith's notes as the Yellow Sequence (and affixed to the extent footage as an addendum). Here, Francis Francine mimes dying in a field of gold enrod as Tiny Tim—then just another Village weirdo, trilling 1920s love songs in MacDougal Street coffeehouses—is filmed perched on an abandoned car in a junkyard beneath the Throg's Neck Bridge, plucking his plastic ukulele. [11]

[11] There were at least two versions of the Yellow Sequence; one, which does not feature Tiny Tim, was shot earlier in the summer, most likely in New Jersey.

Normal Love IS SUMPTUOUS BUT STATIC—IN PART BECAUSE Smith never completed editing it. Although he replied affirmatively when asked by Gerard Malanga, at the conclusion of the undated interview published in *Film Culture* NO. 45 (1968), whether *Normal Love* was finished, this most likely means that he was no longer shooting the movie.

DAVID SACHS, WHO JOINED the production with the cake sequence, recalls that the Swing, Party, and Green scenes had already been shot and that the Blue Scene and the Swamp Sequence were filmed later that summer: "I don't remember ever returning twice to the same location...While there were only a handful of days of filming, there were many more days of hanging around." To judge from the handful of surviving financial records, the first *Normal Love* work print was generated in August 1963 although the shoot continued into October and, in the case of the Moon Pool sequence, through December. There is also evidence of an edge-numbered work print that, in any case, was lost and had to be replaced in late January 1964. [12]

[12] David Sachs, e-mail to J.H. (10/9/2000); Sachs (9/29/2000), OP.CIT.

At the same time that Jonas Mekas was writing checks for the production's raw stock and lab work he covered the cost of printing *Overstimulated* in a check dated August 7, 1963.

ONE CAN ONLY SPECULATE on Smith's plans for the *Normal Love* soundtrack. A small item in *The Village Voice* (10/24/63) announced a grand competition for the *Normal Love* soundtrack:

If you are able to reasonably duplicate the voice of Maria Montez, you are invited to submit a tape recording of the following quote: "Every time I look into the mirror I could scream because I am so beautiful."

Normal Love
frame enlargement
(MARIO MONTEZ, second from left;
ANDY WARHOL, second from right)

SMITH'S NOTES SPECIFY BOTH "African drums" and "classical elation" for the Swing Scene, a "Sol's piano music" as well as "violin and drumming delirium" for the Blue Scene, and a number of specific rural sound effects (insect rustlings, bird calls, frog croaks) for the Swamp Sequence and Party Scene. There are, in addition, references to Hoagy Carmichael's *Monkey Song*, the Patsy Cline song *Walkin' After Midnight*, and the Portuguese singer Amália Rodrigues whose LP *Amália Rodrigues Sings Fado & Flamenco* was, Sachs recalled, constantly played at Joan and Robert Adler's 14TH Street apartment, where Smith and Stanley Alboum also lived. [13]

[13] Sachs (9/29/2000), OP.CIT.

Normal Love
frame enlargement
(TONY CONRAD, foreground;
DIANE DI PRIMA, top right)

SMITH EXHIBITED *Normal Love* rushes and rough cuts through 1965, and thereafter showed excerpts in various combinations with different sorts of exotic musical accompaniment as a projection-performance piece. Thus, like Sergei Eisenstein's unfinished *Que Viva Mexico!* and various Orson Welles projects, *Normal Love*'s extant 125 minutes can only exist as a presentation of footage. [14]

[14] Jerry Tartaglia's restoration is an assemblage of already-edited sequences, with a chronology based on notes made by Smith and Tony Conrad in 1963–64. As these do not include the Yellow Sequence (discovered on a separate reel), it is presented as an addendum. The restored version makes use of selections from Smith's record collection—many of them used during his various in-person presentations of the footage.

Smith's sometime projection of the material, shot at 24 fps, at the slower silent speed (16 fps), as well as his penchant for lengthy reel changes and other projection breakdowns—not to mention the subjective, perhaps pharmaceutically enhanced state of the audience—likely accounts for descriptions of the movie as a four-hour epic.

In his lecture "The Perfect Queer Appositeness of Jack Smith" (9/24/99; STEIRISCHER HERBST, GRAZ, AUSTRIA), Tartaglia notes that with such live film performances, Smith "violated the most sacred convention of cinema" by intruding into "the one place where the filmmaker is not ever supposed to be: the projection situation."

The lore of Jack Smith is replete with both hilarious and terrifying anecdotes of these performances. Sometimes he would make impossible demands of the theater manager and explode in a rage when the management would refuse to repaint the entire theater in a new color immediately. Or he would fixate upon some unfortunate person in the audience and demand that they leave or the show would be cancelled. In the performances in which he advertised the presentation of a film, he would project reels of film material from one of the three feature films, *Flaming Creatures*, *Normal Love*, and *No President*; and to this he would add various shorts and extraneous "scenes", as he labeled them. (Such as the "Yellow Scene," "the Crocodile Scene," etc.) But he wouldn't simply project this film material in a straightforward manner. There would also be live performance, slides, records, and the ever-present disruption of Jack himself, protesting against the horror and failure of the event. He would sometimes remove the full take-up reel from the projector, add or excise certain material, and then re-project it to the unsuspecting audience.

[15] Ron Rice's no-budget first feature, the talk of the Lower East Side during the summer of 1962, provided Smith with a non-Hollywood precedent for *Flaming Creatures*. The beatnik film par excellence, *The Flower Thief* featured coffeehouse poet (and former stockbroker) Taylor Mead as a kind of Zen village idiot, dragging an outsized teddy bear in a child's red wagon as he wandered through the fleshpots of San Francisco's North Beach. Affect alternating between the wistfully infantile and dementedly fey, Mead clowns around sites ranging from jazz bars and downtown street corners to the old Playland amusement park and a vast derelict loft.

The Flower Thief was shot on outdated army surplus 16mm film stock with a handheld camera. The soundtrack was cobbled together out of jazz, Mozart, blues guitar, and children's records, along with some severely sub-Kerouac poetic ravings.

Unscripted and genuinely haphazard, filled with goofy non sequiturs and ultimately less talented than persistent, it was praised by Jonas Mekas in *The Village Voice* as exhibiting "the utmost disrespect for the professional camera, plots, character conventions."

In addition to the numerous positive drug references ("holy holy holy methedrine"), *The Flower Thief* is enlivened by several instances of visual blasphemy, including Mead mooning the camera or wearing the American flag, a nude couple in the shower, and a group of scruffy beatniks restaging the Iwo Jima tableaux.

Chumlum

RON RICE, 1964, 26 MINS. COLOR.

WITH: Jack Smith, Beverly Grant, Mario Montez, Joel Markman, Francis Francine, Guy Henson, Barry Titus, Zelda Nelson, Gerard Malanga, Barbara Rubin, and Frances Stillman.

MUSIC: Angus MacLise.   RECORDING: Tony Conrad.
SPECIAL ASSISTANCE: Stanley Alboum.

SHOWN SUCCESSFULLY AT THE CHARLES DURING THE summer of 1962 Ron Rice's *The Flower Thief* provided Smith with inspiration for *Flaming Creatures*. [15]

Shown at the Charles as part of the June 1962 Filmmakers Festival (which named Rice "most promising filmmaker"), *The Flower Thief* began playing a continuous engagement at the Charles along with another Taylor Mead vehicle, Vernon Zimmerman's *To L.A. with Lust*. Unexpectedly, Rice's feature received something close to a rave from *New York Times* critic Eugene Archer and, despite the Charles's lack of air-conditioning, played to full houses for three weeks.

Thanks to this success, Mead (subsequently described by Brendan Gill in *The New Yorker* as "a cross between a zombie and a kewpie [who] speaks as if his mind and mouth were full of marshmallow") became the first underground movie star, while Smith would later maintain that *Flaming Creatures* was made specifically for the Charles.

In an interview with Jack Sargent, Taylor Mead explained his absense from *Flaming Creatures*:

> I was supposed to be in *Flaming Creatures*, but I already had my *Flower Thief* image so I thought... and I heard there was nudity in *Flaming Creatures*, so I thought "well, I have this image." I was like a young actor "I have this image I must maintain," you know. So I goofed on being in *Flaming Creatures*, which was such a great film, but Jack did once have me playing the violin in front of the screen until the audience began objecting.

Naked Lens: Beat Cinema (LONDON: CREATION BOOKS, 1997), P.84.

A YEAR LATER, RICE RETURNED the compliment. According to P. Adams Sitney, "Rice often accompanied Smith as he was shooting *Normal Love*. They tended to return to [Rice's Canal Street] loft with most of the cast, still in their costumes, after the day's filming. At first Rice made some casual film studies of the actors swinging on the hammocks in his loft. Later he expanded them into the production of *Chumlum*." [16]

[16] *Visionary Film: The American Avant-Garde 1943–1978*, second edition (NEW YORK: OXFORD UNIVERSITY PRESS, 1979), PP. 358–59.

AN ALTOGETHER MORE LANGUID harem movie than *Flaming Creatures*, *Chumlum*—which would be Rice's first and only color film—makes elaborate use of multiple superimpositions, all produced in the camera, and an equally layered soundtrack. Exterior locations include the wrecked car and field of goldenrods that served as the location for *Normal Love*'s Yellow Sequence, as well as a cabin in the woods. "If there is a development or progress in the film," Sitney writes,

It is from indoors to outdoors, from swinging, crawling, and dancing in the harem to dancing in the sky over Coney Island (through superimposition)—an image would recalls the end of The Flower Thief where Taylor Mead dissolves into the sea.

SITNEY SUGGESTS THAT *Chumlum* is meant to be "a reverie in which time is stretched or folded over itself" perhaps within the mind of Smith, who appears in Arabian garb midway through and can be seen sliding around crushing Beverly Grant in a hammock. [17]

17 IBID., P.359.

According to Joan Adler's memoir, *Chumlum* was shot "towards the end of the summer, when the non-stop effort was over and the shooting of *Normal Love* had become sporadic.

Ron's set was ready for *Chumlum*. Jack's creatures set free, Joel, Beverly, Frankie, Rene, Jack himself. They were three-day shooting sessions which led to despair on the creatures' part, two days of waiting for Ron to start shooting, left totally to their own character building and action devices, drained of energy until they slowly emerged into slow, curving dancers in sequence shot over sequence, intermeshing blacks and reds and yellows, curving fabric lines, swaying arms, hair, bodies. Jack started everyone off into make-up and costumes, then started his own. It took three days to finish that, too, as everyone explored the heaps around. Beverly in the hammock.

"ON LOCATION," OP.CIT., P.13.

SUCH FEATURED ROLES WERE commonplace in the underground movies of the mid 1960s. Smith subsequently appeared to extravagant effect opposite Mead in Rice's unfinished epic *The Queen of Sheba Meets the Atom Man* (1963); was included in Andy Warhol's *50 Fantastics and 50 Personalities* (1963–64); played Vincent Van Gogh in Dov Lederberg's *Eargogh* (1964–65), Orpheus in Gregory Markopolous's *Illiac Passion* (1964–66), Jack the Ripper in Bill Vehr's *Brothel* (1966), and either Batman or Dracula in an unfinished film begun by Warhol during the summer of 1964. [18]

18 Smith's other performances of the period include Carl Linder's *Skin* (1964) and *The Devil is Dead* (1964), Naomi Levine's *Jeremelu* (1964), George Kuchar's *Lovers of Eternity* (1964), Piero Heliczer's *Satisfaction* (1966), and various untitled films by Jerry Jofen.

Nô President set photograph,
Jack Smith, circa 1968.
(JEANNE PHILLIPS, left;
MARIO MONTEZ, right rear;
SUSANNA DE MARIA, right)

President

[1] These are the credits advertised for *Nô President*'s February 2, 1969, Elgin screening. A review in *The East Village Other* (2/9/69) cites Charles Henri Ford in the cast. Other uncredited participants, identified by viewers or cited in Smith's production notes, include Tosh Carillo, Francis Francine, John Hawkins, Piero Heliczer, Gerard Malanga, Joel Markman, Jeanne Phillips, and Gaby Rodgers.

No President

1967–70, 50 MINS. SOUND ON TAPE.

WITH: Irving Rosenthal (WENDELL WILLKIE), Doris Desmond (THE LOVE BANDIT), Mario Montez, Donna Kerness, Allegra, Gay Martini, Bill Fortenberry, Jerry Sims, Robert Lavigne, John Vaccaro, Nan King, Ruby Zinnia, Tally Brown, Wendell Willkie, White Pussy, Lob Loach, Yusef. [1]

*T*HE LAST OF JACK SMITH'S 16MM FEATURES— austerely black and white, more an exercise in sensibility than craft—*No President* evolved out of his 1967 program, *Horror and Fantasy at Midnight*, shown first November 9 and 14, 1967, at the New Cinema Playhouse on West 42ND Street (where *Chelsea Girls* had begun its epochal run the year before).

SMITH'S POSTER CITES A NUMBER of individual titles—"film clips from the subterranean chambers of Dr. Madman!"—including *Reefers of Technicolor Island, Scrub-woman of Atlantis* (both in "Livid Color!!"), *Rate droppings of Uranus, Marshgas of Flatulandia, The Flake of Soot*, and *Overstimulated*— shown to the accompaniment of a taped soundtrack by the Cineola Orchestra.

No President set photograph,
Jack Smith, circa 1968.
(MARIO MONTEZ, left)

JONAS MEKAS'S REVIEW IN *The Village Voice* (11/16/67) describes a two-hour-plus presentation of three untitled films, each approximately 45 minutes long.

The first one starred a most beautiful marijuana plant, a gorgeous blooming white queen with her crown reaching towards the sky. In the second part we saw a gallery of Jack's creatures, and there is no other name for them but to call them Jack Smith's creatures. Although they are enacted by other talented and beautiful people, it's Jack's imagination that crowns them with those fantastic gowns and hats and plumes and colors. The third part is like a continuation of the second, but it's in black and white, or more truly, in gray and white.

2 *Movie Journal: The Rise of a New American Cinema, 1959–1971* (NEW YORK: COLLIER BOOKS, 1972), PP. 298–99.

THE MONOCHROMATIC FOOTAGE, Mekas wrote, was no less "glorious and maybe even more so" than the preceding films. To see, Smith's new work, was "like a national holiday." [2]

LIKE KEN JACOBS'S *Star Spangled to Death, Horror and Fantasy at Midnight* would mix original material with found footage. By the time James Stoller saw the program, Smith's 1960 *Overstimulated* was intercut with newsreel footage of the 1940 Republican Convention that nominated Wendell Willkie to run for president. The Willkie footage was projected in and out of focus. "I don't know what Wendell Willkie means to Jack Smith, but I was immoderately moved by this strange juxtaposition," Stoller wrote. The Cineola Orchestra's "haunting" musical accompaniment was now augmented by "some comparably haunting word music, and a gummy Vietnam discourse" which Stoller recalled from

3 "16mm," *The Village Voice* (12/7/67), P.37. Appearing three weeks after Mekas's review, Stoller's piece was written partially in response to a letter published in the *Voice* that had attacked Mekas as "odious" and "reprehensible" for praising Smith.

Smith's 1965 performance *Rehearsal for the Destruction of Atlantis*. These, he thought, invited the audience "to consider the footage of exotic beings, Christmas snow falling, etc. in a considerably wider context. And it's not difficult to do." [3]

JOSEPH ALIAGA'S ACCOUNT HAS has the program open with *Reefers of Technicolor Island*, the same color footage described by Mekas, accompanied by "tooty flutes" and "the ominous tom-tom of drums." Then came color footage of "boys in drag" accompanied by the Vietnam tape.

Seated and languidly swaying with a big fan in front of his-her face the top chief, called Lobster Man, jerks the exposed penis of a faceless naked man standing off to the side while a narrator appropriately touches, in diplomatic terms, on a corrupt official's jerking off a nation, a people, a power and it's funny.

No President
set photograph,
Jack Smith, circa 1968.

THIS WAS FOLLOWED BY "headlights of cars moving at night through rising steam through rising steam from the city's streets," the sequence referred to by Smith as *Marshgas of Flatulandia*; black-and-white interiors of various creature, and, finally, the *Overstimulated* Republican Convention described by Stoller. The last shot, Aliaga wrote, was "a brilliant intuitive leap... a newsreel clip showing hundreds of civilians lined up on both sides of a street wildly cheering army recruits marching off into World War One." [4]

ADVERTISED IN *The Village Voice* (1/18/68) as "Jack Smith's first program since *Flaming Creatures*," *Horror and Fantasy* moved downtown for a five-day run at Aldo Tambellini's Black Gate theater on Second Avenue at 10TH Street. Irving Rosenthal, "author of the Flamboyante new esoteric novel *Sheeper* and first actor to appear on the American screen in glitter makeup," was announced as the star. By late March, this program (still at the Gate) had coalesced into *Kidnapping and Auctioning of Wendell Wilkie* [sic] *by the*

[4] "Jack Smith's Mixed Bag and Then...," *Medium 2* (WINTER 1967–68), PP.33–35.

[5] Irving Rosenthal's novel *Sheeper* was published by Grove Press in January 1968, its cover graced by Smith's portrait of the turbaned author. (Smith's passion for Maria Montez is cited, without particular sympathy, on page 204.) As *No President* evolved, Smith used his Rosenthal portrait to advertise the film.

Other personnel listed in the ad for the January 17–21 run include Mona Joy, Robert Lavigne, Doris, Hakim Kahn, Tiffany Zenobia, Suzanne [sic] de Maria, Allegra, Mario Montez, Gerry [sic] Sims, Wendell Wilkie [sic] and the Lobster. The films were evidently accompanied by John Vaccaro's narration and Angus MacLise's Cineola Orchestra. When *Kidnapping and Auctioning of Wendell Wilkie by the Love Bandit* was presented at the Gate the following March 28, the announced cast was Irving Rosenthal, Doris Desmond, Mario Montez, Donna Kerness, John Lavigne, John Vaccaro, Nan King, Tally Brown, Ruby Zinnia, Bill Fortenberry, and Jerry Sims.

Manny Farber's description of the Gate may be considered definitive:

Tambellini's paradise, the Gate, on Second Avenue, starts as an entrance to an old apartment house, moves through a 1920's marble hallway, and engulfs the customer in a black chamber. God help him. The big sensation here is the ancient unreliable floor, which, like the ceiling in this blitzed miniature cathedral, is indescribable. Sometimes, the shredded carpeting, with its patches of masking tape, feels as spongy and sandy as the beach at Waikiki. Actually, it is an old room of murky origins, painted flat black, no two dimensions the same. There is a bombed-out area in the front half, which houses the screen, and a number of wooden constructions that have been started by a nonunion carpenter and then thrown up as a bad job.

"Experimental Films," *Negative Space: Manny Farber on the Movies* (NEW YORK: DA CAPO, 1998), p.246.

Love Bandit—an all black-and-white presentation starring writer Irving Rosenthal, lipsticked and unshaven, as the infant Wendell abducted by a mustachio'd pirate and sold on the block of a slave market. [5]

ACCORDING TO STOLLER, WHO described the presentation in *The Village Voice*, the show began with "the playing of a Willkie address, in the deep booming tones of old radios." Because Smith typically projected his newsreel footage at silent speed, while leaving the exciter lamp on, the voice-over took on a compelling sluggish tone. "The announcer's voice is slowed down at length until it sounds just like Jack Smith's. Then campaign footage of Willkie on the farm, etc. Then without warning, right into Smith's creatures."

THE CINEOLA ORCHESTRA WAS no longer in evidence. (Indeed, its leader Angus MacLise had just been busted for pot while passing through Oklahoma City.) Instead, Stoller wrote, the images were accompanied by "hoary, familiar music so dumb sounding that even ["nostalgia" disc jockey] Don Ameche wouldn't play it."

Also throughout, the voice of Jack Smith may be heard booming from the projection booth, complaining about one thing or another. He seemed, I thought, to grow most unhappy whenever something particularly beautiful appeared on the screen as if embarrassed by his own powers. [6]

Kidnapping and Auctioning of Wendell Wilkie by the Love Bandit was playing at the Gate when Lyndon Johnson announced that he would not run for a second term as president. This juxtaposition of Smith's Baghdad and American electoral politics proved prophetic. In the summer of 1968, lame-duck LBJ nominated Supreme Court Justice Abe Fortas to replace retiring Earl Warren and, by way of drawing attention to the nominee's liberal position on obscenity, Strom Thurmond organized a "Fortas Film Festival," including *Flaming Creatures*.

[6] "16mm," *The Village Voice* (4/4/69), P.49.

*T*HE FIRST SUNDAY MORNING IN FEBRUARY 1969, LESS THAN two weeks after Richard Nixon's inauguration, an hour-long version of *No President* was shown at the Elgin: "Wendell Wilkie... More Famous Than Most Presidents—He Had Farms in Indiana, Vegatative Motility, and a Willingness to be President..." read the flyer, which also noted "If one knew what one expected of one's president one wouldn't need a president would one?" People thought they knew what was expected on Jack Smith. Andrew Sarris in *The Village Voice* and the reviewer for *The East Village Other* both commented on the size of the crowds. [7]

THE SCREENING WAS CLEARLY an event. Sarris, who attributed his presence to "a spirit of morbid, perhaps even masochistic curiosity," and later wrote a two-part review of a film he clearly hated, put the running time at slightly more than an hour. The footage, including that of Wendell Willkie, was shown silently, with sound provided by "a fatuous Lowell Thomas commentary on the Congo and mood music by Tschaikowsky." [8]

WHERE THE SARRIS REVIEW is near pathological in its ambivalence, Parker Tyler would hail *No President* as "an even more daring exploitation of the themes in *Flaming Creatures* (minus cunnilingual rape and plus political burlesque)" and Mekas reported in the *Voice* (2/13/69) that at least one viewer at the Elgin screening found *No President* "a remarkable first public screening of a film made 50 years ago." [9]

[7] "Films in Focus," *The Village Voice* (2/6/69) P.55; *East Village Other* (2/7/69) N.P. The movie's title is sometimes given as *No President?* Other titles found in Smith's notes include *Wendell Wilkie When Will You Remember to Empty Your Artificial Bladder Before Bedwetting Time?* and *Marshmallow President.* (Smith consistently spells Willkie with one "L," as to some—but not all—commentators on the film.)

[8] "Films in Focus," *The Village Voice* (2/6/69) P.55; "Films in Focus," *The Village Voice* (2/13/69) P.58.

[9] *Underground Film: A Critical History* (NEW YORK: DA CAPO PRESS, 1995) P.42; "Movie Journal," *The Village Voice* (2/13/69) P.57.

No President HAD A MOVE-over run, beginning Friday, February 7, at Cinema 7 "a private club devoted to films for the male homosexual." The same day, a conference on censorship and pornography held on the Notre Dame campus in South Bend, Illinois never got beyond its opening day—disrupted by sheriff's deputies who maced students in breaking up a screening of Andrew Noren's *Kodak Ghost Poems* which, along with *Flaming Creatures* (yanked from the projector after two scandalizing minutes), had been banned by the administration.

ON OCTOBER 30, 1969, *No President* opened for a midnight run at the same Bleecker Street Cinema where *Flaming Creatures* had begun its scarlet career 6½ years before. The film was shown once more, on October 12, 1970, projected in the back room at Max's Kansas City as part of the first New York Underground Film Festival. The lone mention appears to be Jonas Mekas's praise, later that month, in *The Village Voice*:

I sit through a commercial movie, and it does nothing to me. It is so far away from the main concerns and passions of the art of cinema today, that it does nothing to me. Then I go to Max's Kansas City, and I see Jack Smith's show, his present version of No President, and the screen suddenly comes to life. Not only comes to life: It moves with such intense and unique imagination that I sit through a hundred minutes [sic] without once being able to detach myself from it. I think Jack managed to put into this movie fifty, sixty, I don't know how many years of screen's mythology, symbology, everything. He distilled it all to the basic images of the unconscious, and in the most subtle way possible. Jack's film is one of cinema's glories. [10]

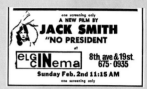

Advertisement,
The Village Voice
(1/3/69)

[10] *Movie Journal*
OP.CIT. P.406.

MEKAS HAD ALREADY WRITTEN to Smith on October 19, 1970, TO inform him that the Selection Committee for the newly-established Anthology Film Archives vote to include both *Flaming Creatures* and *No President* in its canon of essential cinema. In his letter, included among Smith's papers, Mekas stipulated the "original version" of *No President* "in the shape you projected it 15 months ago" as well as the first version of *Flaming Creatures*.

THE SURVIVING VERSION OF *No President* ALTERNATES SCENES shot in Smith's Greene Street loft with found footage— including a Lowell Thomas travelogue of Sumatra, a clip, apparently from the late 1940s, of an unidentified couple singing *A Sunday Kind of Love*, and newsreel footage of candidate Willkie addressing the Future Farmer of America.

THE NARRATIVE IS STRUCTURED around two tableaux. In the first, the future presidential candidate (IRVING ROSENTHAL) is attended by a nurse and then abducted from his crib by a mustachioed pirate (DORIS DESMOND) out of a Spanish galleon flick; in the second, which features a professional belly-dancer as well as the singer Tally Brown striking an agitated diva pose, Willkie is auctioned and sold on the block of a slave market modeled on the one in the 1942 Maria Montez vehicle, *Arabian Nights*. Thus, Smith's hothouse childhood fantasies merge with entropic, harshly lit glamour scenes wherein the garishly costumed hobnob with the brazenly nude. As befits a political scenario, *No President* is rife with representations of the phallus—metaphoric and otherwise. Among other things, the movie literalizes the idea of a champagne cocktail.

IN AN UNPUBLISHED MEMOIR, Charles Bergengren recalls that *No President* was preceded by the color short subject *Song for Rent*. Here, Smith appeared as his red-wigged, plastic-jawed, alter ego Rose Courtyard, seated in a wheelchair amid detritus of his Greene Street loft. The film was accomplished by two renditions of Kate Smith singing *God Bless America*. Dressed in a red satin gown, clutching a bouquet of dead roses, Rose is finally moved to stand up and salute. 11

Advertisement, *The Village Voice* (4/22/71).

11 Smith's papers included a monologue written for Rose Courtyard, complete with stage directions:

Hello, I'm Rose Courtyard. Deep down inside of me [laff] I'm a very patriotic girl. Last night on the Celebrity Beanbag program I was given the humility award for my [with mongolian pride] NINETEENTH PLANE CRASH!!! You may have noticed my plastic jaw— and as you can see my dancing days are over. Aren't these roses beautiful? Roses have always been identified with me as all my fans know—that is my real fans, not just bloodsuckers. Here's my photo album, my scrapbook right here. Let me tell you about some of my plane crashes. I've had quite a few plane crashes—the last one was going to entertain our boys. Their LIVES DEPEND ON keeping the war going! Their lives depend on it... actually my song was ended by a few bad roles—but [thoughtful, serious] my career was finally undoubtedly ended when a sightseeing bus I was on was smashed into by a helicopter on the New Jersey TURNPIKE!

I'm going to sing a song for you...

SONG

That bottle. Oh—it fell— Oh let me pick it it [sic] — on SHIT COCK suck— fuck you!! Motherfuck OH SHIT—GOD BLESS CONSTRUCTION WORKERS.

Respectable Creatures

Untitled "plastique,"
Jack Smith, circa 1962.
(MARIAN ZAZEELA, left;
FRANCIS FRANCINE, right)

I was a
Male Yvonne
De Carlo

Respectable Creatures

1950S; 1966, 35 MINS. COLOR. SOUND ON TAPE.
A.K.A. *Buzzards Over Bagdad, Loathsome Kisses of Bagdad, Normal Fantasy*

*J*ACK SMITH'S "LIVE FILMS" MIGHT INCORPORATE footage going back to the mid 1950s. Thus, *Respectable Creatures* intercuts material from Smith's first movie, *Buzzards Over Bagdad*, with scenes shot over a decade later during carnival in Rio de Janeiro.

[1] Smith screened the footage for Ronald Tavel during the 1960s, commissioning Tavel—who believes the material was shot in Los Angeles—to write intertitles, which were never used. (RONALD TAVEL, UNPUBLISHED INTERVIEW, 8/24/94.)

The title *Buzzards over Bagdad* was recycled in 1966 for the "underground movie flip book" included the December 1966 issue of *Aspen*, a box magazine co-edited by Andy Warhol.

Announced as coming from "the forthcoming film *Buzzards over Bagdad*, a Cinemaroc North African Nicolodeon Presentation by Jack Smith," the images appear to be frame enlargements from black-and-white footage that would later be incorporated in *No President*.

"Once and only once [Jack] showed me the thing he'd been shooting in the loft in the 20's before we met," Ken Jacobs wrote in unpublished letter to *The Village Voice* (10/21/91).

It was very promising in crazy way, totally blind, totally sincere. And almost entirely taking place in his head, the screen image no more than stimulant for his head-trip. He'd built a foot-high pool of water in a raw industrial loft, gather fronds to it and conned/coerced this poor stringy nervous girl into simulating Maria Montez narcissism against the glare of a point-blank floodlight. Attempting, humorlessly, witlessly, Hollywood-straightforwardly but ineptly to achieve The Beautiful as he'd become acquainted with in Wisconsin.

THE EXTANT FOOTAGE OF THE 16MM film, which Smith may have begun in the early 1950s while living in Los Angeles and was apparently still shooting when he first met Ken Jacobs in 1956, suggests a relatively straightforward gloss on the Maria Montez vehicle *The Arabian Nights*—specifically drawing upon a scene that involves a harem girl and her lover putting poison in the caliph's wine. [1]

JACOBS REGARDED SMITH'S intentions as devoid of irony— although that was certainly not the case a decade or more later when Smith intercut *Buzzards over Bagdad* with bits of *Normal Love* and documentary footage taken, in February 1966, of Rio slums and street urchins. [2]

DISCOVERED IN A FILM CAN labeled *Respectable Creatures*, a version of this composition, also incorporating material from *I Was a Male Yvonne De Carlo*, was shown in 1983 at the Millennium in New York under the rubric *Normal Fantasy*. The posthumous version is accompanied by tapes made by Smith in Brazil which were in the possession of Jerry Lieber.

[2] Smith's trip to Rio was sponsored by songwriter Jerry Leiber and his wife, the actress Gaby Rodgers, best remembered for her performance as the fatal woman in Robert Aldrich's *Kiss Me Deadly*. In an undated letter written to Leiber from Brazil, Smith explains that his original plans to make a travelogue have "expanded" into a dramatic movie that will use the carnival as its starting point. Smith's papers include a shot list for a film called *Carnaval* [sic] *in Lobsterland*.

Flipbook, Jack Smith, produced for *Aspen Magazine*. (DECEMBER 1966)

I Was a Male Yvonne De Carlo

EDITED BY JACK SMITH
RELEASED 1998. 30 MINS. B&W. AND COLOR.
SOUND ON TAPE BY JERRY TARTAGLIA

SHOT MAINLY DURING THE LATE '60S AND EDITED a decade or more later, *I Was a Male Yvonne De Carlo* (as the can in which it was discovered was labeled) is one of several films and slide-shows in which the artist features himself as a mock celebrity—its title recalling Smith's early '80s performance piece, *I Was a Male Yvonne De Carlo for the Lucky Landlord Underground.* [3]

[3] In 1945, after Walter Wanger cast her in *Salome, Where She Danced*, the soulless, plastic Yvonne De Carlo replaced Maria Montez as Universal's Queen of Technicolor and reigning babe of mishigas. Unlike "The Wonderful One," as Ron Tavel writes, De Carlo "cherished no secret 'art' ambitions and gave the studio few headaches. And, if she had no magic, no tangi-ble passion, no leg-endary superstructure, well, that was the age Hollywood was moving into." According to Tavel, Smith felt that, by the mid 1970s, the Lower East Side had entered a De Carlo age, second-rate and inauthentic, "stuck in the gummy cobwebs covering the real thing."

I also had the feeling that he said Miss De Carlo as one says 'Gee' rather than Jesus, or 'Gosh' and 'Golly' rather than God. And when I'd confront the neologist with that suspicion, he'd shyly, even humbly agree. I was not wise to tempt the minatory gods with continual familiarity.

In an unpublished interview with Callie Angell and myself (8/24/94), Tavel elaborated.

When [Jack] would talk a great deal about Yvonne De Carlo, I'd say, "Well, why do you talk so much about her?" And he'd say, "You can't get the real thing anymore and it's better to deal with removal and displacement."

Tavel believes that Wanger had De Carlo in the chorus line as early as *Arabian Nights* (1942) as a possible Montez replacement and that this threat was actually made during the shooting of *Sudan* (1945), Montez's last Technicolor film for Universal.

Jack Smith
publicity photograph
circa 1970.

THE MOVIE OPENS WITH THE excerpt from *No President* originally called *Marsh Gas of Flatulandia*—several minutes of black-and-white footage of steam escaping manholes segues to an interior scene of various creatures emerging from dry ice vapors—then shifts to color to show the filmmaker, clad in a leopard-skin jumpsuit, attended by a nurse as he sits amidst the detritus of his duplex loft on Grand and Greene Street.

SMITH WAITS UNDER THE visible movie lights, drumming his fingers. A fan presents him with a black-and-white glamour shot (Smith in profile, posed with a sinuously curved dagger) to autograph as the Warhol superstar Ondine, dressed entirely in black leather, snaps his picture. Violence erupts as the nurse takes out a whip to discipline the star's fans. When a female creature pulls out the same dagger depicted in the glamour shot, Smith jumps up and shakes the weapon from her hand. The action is post-scripted with footage of a steam shovel patrolling the rubble where a 14TH Street movie palace once stood.

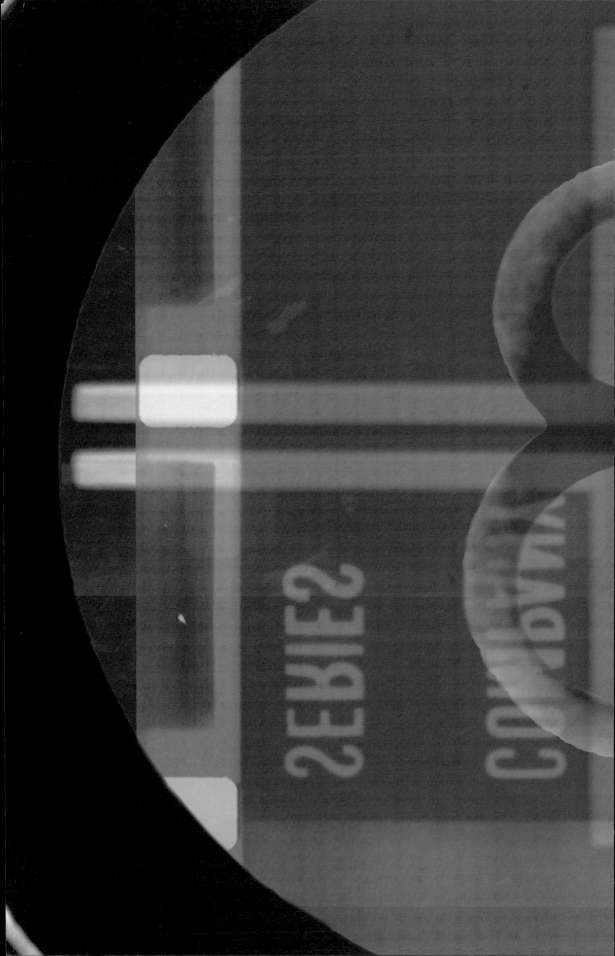

Appendices

Jack Smith on 8mm

JACK SMITH'S FIRST MOVIES WERE MADE IN 8MM. Ken Jacobs recalls seeing

The charming, all-heart 8mm movie [Jack] shot in his early teens, The Saracens, for which his mother had sewn costumes for the neighborhood kids and in which the roofs of neighboring suburban homes loom clearly over the strung cloths penning in his Bagdad. [1]

UNFORTUNATELY, LIKE contemporary 8mm juvenilia by the filmmakers Kenneth Anger and Gregory Markopoulous, Smith's Kenosha, Wisconsin, peplum appears to have been lost.

SMITH STARRED IN SEVERAL narrow-gauge productions. In 1965, he appeared, along with several other underground filmmakers and a monstrous cockroach, in George Kuchar's burlesque of bohemian squalor, *The Lovers of Ecstasy*. Fifteen years later, Smith lent his presence to a subsequent Lower Manhattan avant-garde—playing the exotic psychiatrist Dr. Shrinklestein in Beth B and Scott B's super-8 sound feature *The Trap Door*. (Within two minutes of his appearance, late in the movie, Smith has changed into Arabian Nights drag and taken control, dangling a pasty jewel in front of the hapless hero's nose and drawling, "Have you ev-ver been... hyyyp-no-tized?" [2])

[1] Ken Jacobs, unpublished letter to *The Village Voice* (10/21/91).

[2] Originally called *The Unclean, Lust for Ecstasy* was shot in an East 12TH Street apartment Smith then shared with Dov Lederberg, also in the movie and "a filmmaker so pretentious and recondite he has even managed to alienate [Jonas] Mekas" per Robert Christgau's piece in the "New York" section of the November 20, 1966, *New York World-Journal Tribune*. *Lust for Ecstasy*, as Kuchar explained it to Christgau, "concerned a poet 'who lacked only one thing—inspiration.'" Christgau noted that the movie was "filled with wildly uncomplimentary shots of Lederberg's refrigerator and his oozing walls."

IN THE INTERIM BETWEEN these two satires of art world innocence, Smith himself switched to super-8 for the making (or not) of *Sinbad in the Rented World*, in which he appeared as the former dancing boy and aspiring radio personality, Sinbad Glick. This may or may not be the "*Arabian Nights* architecture film" to which Smith refers in his 1978 interview with Sylvére Lotringer or the 20-minute assemblage (not yet preserved) that, labeled *Sinbad of Bagdad*, was shot on the wintry Coney Island beach sometime during the late 1970s. A group of well-swaddled creatures, including a mother and baby, line up in formation. Some of their costumes sport papier-mâché phalluses. The mise-en-scène also includes miniature animals, empty bottles of Bali Hai wine, and an advertisement for Preparation H. These staged scenes are interspersed with verite footage taken of the crowds around Surf Avenue. [3]

SMITH ALSO LEFT A NUMBER of super-8 camera rolls. One of these features a particularly striking appearance by the Lobster in full regalia. Another half dozen rolls, seemingly from the same project, appear to have been shot by Smith himself in the early 1970s amid the detritus of his Greene Street loft. Two later rolls, including *Putting Litter in Pool* (1977), present Smith performing on the Mall in Washington, DC, at the time of the National Gallery's enormously popular Tutankhamen exhibit.

[3] Smith's papers describe *Sinbad* in some detail, e.g., "in the confusion of the climactic roach stampede, the Lobster in his final priestly disguise with the forehead earring of exoticism in his back pocket, is drowned in Plaster Lagoon." See *Wait for Me at the Bottom of the Pool: The Writings of Jack Smith*, ed. J. Hoberman and Edward Leffingwell (LONDON: SERPENT'S TAIL, 1997), PP.146–47.

Jack Smith, frame enlargement
Little Stabs at Happiness,
Ken Jacobs, 1959–63

Jacobs • Fellini • Warhol

Saturday Afternoon Blood Sacrifice

KEN JACOBS, 1957, 4 MINS. WITH BOB FLEISCHNER AND
JACK SMITH. B&W. SILENT.

Little Cobra Dance

KEN JACOBS, 1957, 2 MINS. WITH JACK SMITH. B&W. SILENT.

Star Spangled to Death

KEN JACOBS, 1958–60, 120 MINS. WITH JACK SMITH AND
JERRY SIMS. COLOR AND B&W.

Star Spangled to Death.
Ken Jacobs, frame enlargement
(JACK SMITH)

Little Stabs at Happiness

K.M. ROSENTHAL (KEN JACOBS), 1959–62, 15 MINS. WITH
JACK SMITH AND JERRY SIMS. COLOR.

Blond Cobra

KEN JACOBS AND BOB FLEISCHNER, 1959–63, 33 MINS.
WITH JACK SMITH. B&W AND COLOR.

The Death of P'town:
A Fragment of a Movie
That Never Was

KEN JACOBS, 1961, 7 MINS. WITH JACK SMITH AS THE
FAIRY VAMPIRE. COLOR. SILENT.

AUDITING A FILMMAKING CLASS AT CITY college in 1956, Jack Smith met the future filmmaker Bob Flieschner and, through Flieschner, his most important aesthetic collaborator, Ken Jacobs.

AN ASPIRING ABSTRACT Expressionist painter, Jacobs prized the immediate and gestural. Like the contemporary forms of Assemblage and Happenings, his early 16mm films extended the action aesthetic into other realms, manifesting a similar involvement with found objects and the urban picturesque. Performing in Jacobs's films, Smith animated derelict landscapes with his manic acting-out and spontaneous clowning—a capacity for what Parker Tyler would describe as the "sloughing off civilized dignity and indulging amoral naked impulses in the sight of all."[1]

[1] *Underground Film: A Critical History* (NEW YORK: DA CAPO, 1995), P.20.

THE FOUR-MINUTE *Saturday Afternoon Blood Sacrifice* and two-minute *Little Cobra Dance*, both black-and-white and silent, were shot on consecutive days during the summer of 1957 with Smith filmed cavorting (and at one point, attracting the attention of the police) in the deserted alleys of lower Manhattan's no-longer extent Washington Market, near Smith's Reade Street loft. Thereafter, throughout 1958 and 1959, Smith was cast as the primary figure in Jacobs's epic *Star Spangled to Death*—a vast, not-yet-completed symphony of social disgust which interpolated all manner of found footage (soft-core porn films, home movies, political advertisements) into scenes of Smith's bizarre clowning—as well as appearing in its unedited (or rather, edited-in-camera) spin-off, the 15-minute *Little Stabs at Happiness*. Both films were shot on the roof and

Jack Smith on the set of *Star Spangled to Death*, Ken Jacobs, circa 1957.

[2] Jacobs initially released *Little Stabs at Happiness* under the pseudonym K.M. Rosenthal. His description in *Film-Makers' Cooperative Catalogue* NO. 3 (1965) reads:

A few of those inexpressible moods of the moment are captured and displayed on film as they never before have been. "In the Gold Room," "It Began to Drizzle," "The Spirit of Listlessness," and others are examples of pure, golden joy. Unedited for addition of titles. Lavish color, unrelated improvisations, the good and the bad. Strictly light summer fare. Very easy and fun to do. Superior in a way to a spite choked feature I've been grinding out for years. A true breather."

[3] IBID., PP.79–80. The period of Jacobs's and Smith's collaboration coincides with a number of parallel artistic endeavors. It was during the summer of 1957 that John Cassavetes began working on *Shadows*; November 1959 when the revised *Shadows* was shown with the world premiere of the Robert Frank, Alfred Leslie, Jack Kerouac collaboration *Pull My Daisy* at Cinema 16. Early 1960 brought *Four Happenings* at the Reuben Gallery and *Ray Gun Spex* at Judson. That same spring, the Bleecker Street and New Yorker revival houses opened. Jonas Mekas began shooting *Guns of the Trees* during the summer of 1960 at a time when Shirley Clarke was working on a film version of *The Connection*. The New American Film-Makers' Group established the Film-Makers' Cooperative in late 1960.

in the courtyard of the West 75TH Street apartment building where Jacobs was employed as superintendent—as well as in various New York junkyards and construction sites. [2]

PARKER TYLER, ONE OF THE few critics to take note of *Star-Spangled to Death*, understood its anticipation of the Oldenburg Happenings of the early 1960s (while tracing its "use of the trash pile as a source of costume and decor" and "infantile-neurotic" mode of acting back to the European avant-garde of Kurt Schwitters).

Star-Spangled to Death is a grimly poetic camp phrase expressing the anti-patriotic radical socialism which, Jacobs believes, was the true impetus of the emergent Underground as distinct from the elder avant-garde. The film shows two beat characters, Jack Smith and a male crony [Jerry Sims], struggling with a life style; Smith represents an ambiguous joie-de-

vivre with manic-depressic roots: wild clowning (en travesti) amid slum surroundings; his friend shows the utterly dour side, withdrawn and "speechless," lacking any of the grotesque theater which makes Smith an "acting personality."

AN AVATAR OF THE NEW Underground in Tyler's opinion, *Star-Spangled to Death* was less interested in shocking the bourgeoisie than providing "a documentary showcase for the underdog's spontaneous, uncontrolled fantasy." [3]

JACOBS IS ALSO RESPONSIBLE for introducing Smith to Joseph Cornell's then-unknown masterpiece *Rose Hobart*, which Cornell lent to Jacobs, his ever-potential studio assistant, in 1960. To make *Rose Hobart*, Cornell had distilled and reshuffled footage from one of his secret-flix, the exotic adventure *East of Borneo* (COLUMBIA, 1931), titling this new and nonlinear film after *East of*

Borneo's female star. Jacobs borrowed *Rose Hobart*'s spliced original as well as the *Holiday in Brazil* record album Cornell used as musical accompaniment, holding onto the film (which had not been publicly screened since its December 1936 premiere at Julien Levy's gallery) for over a year while he and Smith subjected it to careful study.

> We looked at it in every possible way: on the ceiling, in mirrors, bouncing it all over the room, in corners, in focus, out of focus, with a blue filter that Cornell had given me, without it, backwards. It was just like an eruption of energy... [4]

THE IMPRESSION THE FILM made on Smith may be deduced from the copy of *The Beautiful Book* he annotated for Marian Zazeela, making reference to "the previously greatest movie on earth, Joseph Cornell's Rose Hobart film."

AS FILM CRITIC AND HISTORIAN P. Adams Sitney was the first to point out, *Flaming Creatures* can be seen as a version of *Rose Hobart*, in which Hollywood secret-flix fantasies are restaged rather than reedited. *Rose Hobart* subsequently evinced itself as an influence on Jacobs's oeuvre with his re-filmed 1905 short *Tom, Tom, the Piper's Son* (1969) as well as in his numerous projection pieces. [5]

JACOBS AND SMITH MADE their last film together, *The Death of P'Town*, in Provincetown during the summer of 1961. Here, Smith appears as the Fairy Vampire, wrapped in a white sheet and cavorting through the old cemetery on the hill behind the Pilgrim Monument. It was during that summer (during which Jacobs met his future wife, Florence Karpf) that Smith came out— to Jacobs, at least—as a homosexual. [6]

[4] *Visionary Film: The American Avant-Garde 1943-1978*, second edition (NEW YORK: OXFORD UNIVERSITY PRESS, 1979), P.349.

[5] IBID.

Jack Smith publicity photograph, circa 1970.

[6] Ken Jacobs, unpublished letter to *The Village Voice* (10/21/91).

7 For a detailed account, see Ken Jacobs's "The Great Blonde Cobra Collaboration," *Wait for Me at the Bottom of the Pool: The Writings of Jack Smith*, ed. J. Hoberman and Edward Leffingwell (LONDON: SERPENT'S TAIL, 1997), PP.162–63. Although Jacobs puts the *Blonde Cobra* premiere on April 29, it was shown previously at the Bleecker, on the night of February 11, as part of Mekas's *Newest Absurd and Zen Poetry* program. At that time, the film was credited solely to Bob Fleischner. Jacobs's finished soundtrack to *Little Stabs at Happiness* (which dates itself February 27, 1963) refers to the February 11 program.

HABITUÉS OF THE CHARLES screenings, Jacobs and Smith were both "discovered" there during the spring of 1962. *Little Stabs at Happiness*, which was shown anonymously to the accompaniment of several ancient 78-rpm records at the Charles on June 6, attracted Jonas Mekas's attention—as did Smith's *Scotch Tape*. *Little Stabs at Happiness* existed only as camera original. When Mekas offered to help Jacobs with his lab bills, the filmmaker alerted him to the existence of another, unfinished Smith project, namely *Blonde Cobra*.

IN EARLY 1959, SMITH HAD collaborated with Fleischner on a "comic horror film." The movie was abandoned after a falling out and the footage turned over to Jacobs, who, without concern for the original intentions, edited it the following winter

into the 33-minute portrait of Smith that would be known as *Blonde Cobra*. In the late spring or early summer of 1962, Jacobs and Smith "struck a truce" (per Jacobs) and assembled a soundtrack that juxtaposed snatches of a Fred Astaire-Ginger Rogers movie, a German tango, a children's record, and taped radio news, with Smith's hysterical sing-song "confessions." 7

SHOWN WITH *Flaming Creatures* at its premiere on April 29, 1963, and frequently paired with it thereafter, *Blonde Cobra* established Smith as an underground star on par with Taylor Mead. (In fact, Ron Rice had already written him into his work-in-progress *The Queen of Sheba Meets the Atom Man*.) The same week, in *The Village Voice*, Jonas Mekas announced the arrival of a "new cinema of disengagement and freedom."

The movies I have in mind are Ron Rice's The Queen of Sheba Meets the Atom Man; Jack Smith's The Flaming Creatures [sic]; Ken Jacobs' Little Stabs at Happiness; Bob Fleischner's Blonde Cobra—four works that make up the real revolution in cinema today. These movies are illuminating and opening up sensibilities and experiences never before recorded in the American arts; a content which Baudelaire, the Marquis de Sade, and Rimbaud gave to world literature a century ago...

Blonde Cobra, MEKAS WROTE, was "the masterpiece of the Baudelairean cinema... a work hardly surpassable in perversity, in richness, in beauty, in sadness, in tragedy." [8]

JACOBS'S DESCRIPTION FOR the Film-Makers' Cooperative Catalogue acknowledges Smith's own dislike for the finished film—which extended into the late 1970s, when he had a lawyer send letters to Jacobs and Fleischner requesting that they cease and desist showing the film.

Blonde Cobra is an erratic narrative—no, not really a narrative, it's only stretched out in time for convenience of delivery. It's a look in on an exploding life, on a man of imagination suffering pre-fashionable lower East Side deprivation and consumed with American 1950s, '40s, '30s disgust. Silly, self-pitying, guilt-strictured and yet triumphing—on one level—over the situation with style, because he's unapologetically gifted, has a genius for courage, knows that a state of indignity can serve to show his character in sharpest relief. He carries on, states his presence for what it is. Does all he can to draw out our condemnation, testing our love for limits, enticing us into an absurd moral posture the better to dismiss us with a regal "screw-off."

[8] *Movie Journal: The Rise of a New American Cinema, 1959–1971* (NEW YORK: COLLIER BOOKS, 1972), PP.85–86.

"*T*WO MINUTES AFTER I MET FEDERICO FELLINI IN ROME," a flabbergasted Stanley Kauffmann reported in *The New Republic* during the winter of 1964, "he asked me whether I'd seen Jack Smith's *Flaming Creatures*." [9]

[9] Stanley Kauffmann, *A World on Film* (NEW YORK: DELTA, 1967), P.424.

[10] *Film Is: The International Free Cinema* (WOODSTOCK NY: OVERLOOK PRESS, 1975) PP.58–59.

FELLINI'S ALLEGED ADMIRATION for Smith was a persistent legend throughout the 1960s. Steve Dwoskin writes that *Flaming Creatures*'s "first screening [sic] took place in a storage loft just off Washington Square Village.

[11] Unpublished interview with Edward Leffingwell, 12/9/94; Parker Tyler, *Screening the Sexes: Homosexuality in the Movies* (NEW YORK: HOLT, RINEHART AND WINSTON, 1972), P.237.

Various members of the press managed to get in and it was rumored that Fellini and a few other 'known' film people were there as well. The seats were planks of wood stretched across boxes, with a few old lavatories that had been stored there also turned into seats. [10]

JONAS MEKAS MAINTAINS THAT he showed both *Flaming Creatures* and *Normal Love* to Fellini, as well as to Michelangelo Antonioni, when they were in New York. Parker Tyler notes that Fellini "saw and admired [*Flaming Creatures*] before he made the *Satyricon*." Specifically, Tyler suggests that *Flaming Creatures*'s "atavistic hommage to the female" and "instinctive sort of monosexuality" is reiterated in "the way in which the black Venus of *Fellini Satyricon*, by virtue of sex magic, rescues the homosexual Encolpius from the impotence that overtakes him." [11]

FREELY ADAPTED FROM PETRONIUS Arbiter's fragmentary first-century burlesque of Roman society, *Fellini Satyricon* is a nearly plotless spectacle—a programatically non-Christian, carnivalesque freak show in which the men are mainly homosexual and the women in a constant state of erotic arousal.

While this quintessential Fellini movie recalls the stone age of the Italian peplum genre, its visions and orgies seem even more an attempt to trump the post-Smith underground movie. *Satyricon* "has the quality of a drug-induced hallucination, being without past or future," Vincent Canby wrote in *The New York Times* (3/14/70), while the anonymous (and less-enthusiastic) reviewer for *Time* (3/16/70) complained that "Encolpius and his colleagues are too much obviously fashioned after contemporary faggots," both writers echoing the tenor of Smith's earlier notices. Fellini himself suggested that his *Satyricon* was a youth-trip along the lines of Kubrick's *2001* and much was made of his casting a hippie found on the streets of London's Chelsea and a member of the New York cast of *Hair* as his leads. [12]

"WATCHING [*Satyricon*], I regretted that Jack Smith never completed *Normal Love*,"

Jonas Mekas wrote in *The Village Voice* (5/14/70).

It was almost painful, just to think that Satyricon is there and Normal Love isn't. It is very possible that Satyricon contains some of Fellini's most imaginative film images. And there is a reality in it, in parts of it, the reality of sad, sentimental, lonely, melodramatic Coney Island and 42nd Street creatures, caught with great love. But it's also one aspect of the world and texture and feeling what Jack Smith dealt with in Normal Love, and in Jack's hands it all became something else: the sadness, the sentimentality, the melodrama, and the abnormality were transcended through Jack's art... [13]

ALTHOUGH SMITH SPENT THE summer of 1974 in Rome (where he exhibited slides at Fabio Sargentini's gallery and created the slide-show *I Danced with a Penguin*), there is no evidence that he and Fellini ever met.

[12] According to his early publicity, Fellini originally conceived *Satyricon* an all-star Hollywood parody featuring such past and present luminaries as Groucho Marx, Jimmy Durante, Terence Stamp, Danny Kaye, and the Beatles. The intention to cast Mae West in major role suggests an avatar of Michael Sarne's *Myra Breckinridge* (1970), another big-budget descendant of *Flaming Creatures*. Alex Chacellor, "Fellini Fun With Classic," *Newark Sunday News* (9/1/68), P.E3.

Satyricon's only known star—and a minor one at that—is the nearly unrecognizable Capuccine. A pity Fellini didn't find a role for Tina Aumont, daughter of Maria Montez, who would appear as one of Donald Sutherland's conquests in *Federico Fellini's Casanova* (1976).

[13] *Fellini Satyricon* would also remind Pauline Kael of an underground movie, although the one she cites—by title, not author—is John Water's 1969 *Mondo Trasho*:

If you have ever been at a high-school play in which the children trying to look evil stuck their tongues out, you'll know exactly why there's so little magic in Fellini's apocalyptic extravaganza. It's full of people making faces, the way people do in home movies, and full of people staring at the camera and laughing and prancing around, the way they often do in sixteen-millimeter parodies of sex epics like Mondo Trasho.

"Fellini's Mondo Trasho," *Deeper into Movies* (BOSTON: ATLANTIC MONTHLY/LITTLE, BROWN, 1973), P.130.

Camp

ANDY WARHOL, 1965, 70 MINS. B&W.

WITH (IN ORDER OF APPEARANCE), Gerard Malanga (HOST), Baby Jane Holzer, Paul Swan, Mario Montez, Mar-Mar, Jody Babb, Tally Brown, Jack Smith, Fufu Smith, Donyle, and Tosh Carillo.

14 Andy Warhol, Andy and Pat Hackett, *POPism: The Warhol '60s* (NEW YORK: HARCOURT BRACE JOVANICH, 1980), PP.31—32.

Warhol is considerably more effusive in an interview with David Ehrenstein published in *Film Culture* NO. 40 (SPRING 1966):

DE: Who in the New American Cinema do you admire?
AW: Jaaaacck Smiiiittth.
DE: You really like Jack Smith?
AW: When I was little, I always... thought he was my best director.... I mean, just the only person I would ever copy, and just.... so terrific and now since I'm grown up, I just think that he makes the best movies.
DE: What in particular do you like about his movies?
AW: He's the only one I know who uses color...backwards. (P.41)

Several of Smith's creatures, most notably Mario Montez, became Warhol superstars. In fact, the coinage "superstar" is Smith's. A selection of his photographs, "Superstars of Cinemaroc," was published in the first issue of *Gnaoua* (SPRING 1964).

*A*NDY WARHOL'S INTEREST IN SMITH'S MOVIES HAS BEEN well documented—not least by Warhol himself. Present for the filming of *Normal Love*'s cake sequence at Eleanor Ward's estate in Old Lyme Connecticut, the artist studied Smith's technique:

I picked something up from him for my own movies—the way he used anyone who happened to be around that day, and also how he just kept shooting until the actors got bored... The preparations for every shooting were like a party— hours and hours of people putting makeup on and getting into costume and building sets.

WARHOL FURTHER NOTED that his second 16mm film was "a little newsreel of the people out there filming for Jack." This three-minute camera roll, *Jack Smith Shooting Normal Love*, was showing with *Flaming Creatures* at the New Bowery when NYPD detectives busted the theater on March 3, 1964. 14

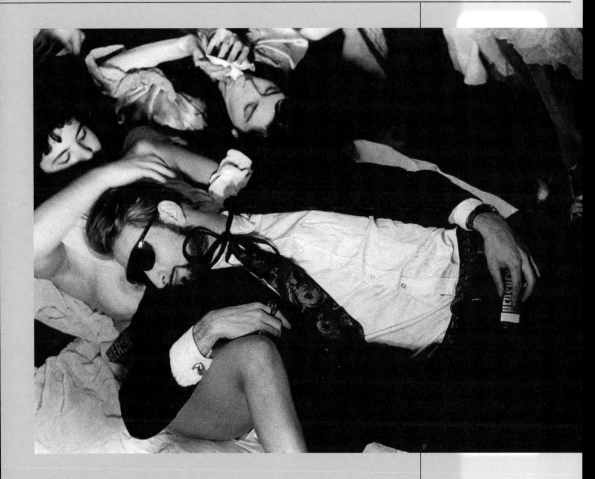

THE UNDERGROUND NEARLY went under during the spring of 1964. There were no more public screenings, as Jonas Mekas devoted his energies to a series of court battles. Smith was unable to complete *Normal Love*, although he continued to show it as rushes. Ken Jacobs could not raise money to finish *Star Spangled to Death*. Ron Rice took off for Mexico, where he died of pneumonia in December 1964. Under the circumstances, the major force in underground movies became Warhol—the one figure who was able to subsidize his own studio.

Jack Smith in the Factory, circa 1964. Unknown photographer.

SMITH'S MAJOR COLLABORATION with Warhol, known variously as *A Lavender Filter Throughout, The Rose Without Thorns, Dracula, Batman Dracula,* and (by Smith) *Rodney Dracula,* is a silent feature— albeit the first Warhol production to use lights—shot, as a series of 100-foot 16mm camera rolls, in the aftermath of the *Flaming Creatures* trial, during the summer of 1964.

SUGGESTING A CROSS BETWEEN a mad scientist's lab and a discotheque, the Factory scenes feature Rufus Collins, Ivy Nicholson, Gerard Malanga, Billy Name, an unidentified male nude, a raw chicken, and Baby Jane Holzer in a tinfoil bikini. The various entanglements, scarcely more risqué than foot kissing, suggest a modified *Flaming Creatures* entanglement. The scene ends as Smith, dressed in black and sporting a pair of Halloween fangs, twists with Beverly Grant atop a mock operating table.

ANOTHER SERIES OF FACTORY interiors features Taylor Mead, Tally Brown, Beverly Grant, Baby Jane Holzer, Gerard Malanga. Smith, again in fangs, lurks about—wrapping Ronnie Cutrone's head in aluminum foil and dancing with his mirrored reflection. A third Factory sequence has a bejeweled Smith first dancing and then playing footsie with a half-dressed Sally Kirkland, who, abruptly ravished by Beverly Grant, walks off abashed and puts on her skirt.

THERE ARE ALSO TWO SERIES of exterior rolls. One, shot on a Long Island estate, shows the caped Smith in long shot, dancing, twirling, running towards camera, and collapsing. Holzer, Nicholson, and Grant are also present—as is Naomi Levine, who is abducted by a naked man. The second has a subdued Smith twirling his cape on the Factory roof in the company of Tally Brown and Beverly Grant—whose picture on the cover of the Summer 1964 *Film Culture* is taken from this sequence. [15]

[15] The credit reads "Beverly Grant on the set of the Rompalmhol Production *A Lavender Filter Throughout (A Concatenation of Jack Smiths)* by Andy Warhol in association with Henry Romney and John Palmer, 1964."

Batman Dracula—AS THE footage has come to be called—was never completed (or even edited), although excerpts were shown at the New Yorker theater on December 7, 1964. [16]

[16] Warhol's account of *Dracula*—"the filming went on for months"—may be found in *POPism*, OP.CIT., PP.32, 70—71.

ON OCTOBER 28, 1965, *Normal Love* was screened at the Film-Makers' Cinematheque on a bill with Warhol's *Temptations*—soon to be retitled *My Hustler*. Two days after the premiere of what would be Warhol's first real popular success, Smith—by now the subject of some 15 Factory "screen tests" as well as a collaborator on at least one unfinished feature—appeared in Warhol's *Camp*.

BASICALLY A FILMED VARIETY program, *Camp* had its premiere at the Film-Makers' Cinematheque on November 18 as part of the two-week New Cinema Festival of shadow plays, slide pieces, psychedelic light shows, and multimedia performances (many quite aggressive in their sensory bombardment) that also included Smith's *Rehearsal for the Destruction of Atlantis*. Warhol, who would unveil his own multimedia extravaganza, *Andy Warhol, Uptight*, two months later at the annual dinner of the New York Society for Clinical Psychiatry, was here a step behind. For the ad that ran in *The Village Voice* (11/18/65) he wrote, "Everyone is being so creative for this festival that I thought I would just show a bad movie. The camera work is so bad, the lighting is awful. The technical work is terrible—but the people are so fantastic."

ALTHOUGH *Camp* IS BARELY acknowledged in the literature on Warhol's movies, filmmaker Thom Andersen gave it an unusually full description in the June 1966 issue of *Artforum*. *Camp*, Andersen wrote, "is essentially one unedited shot, interrupted by one reel change."

As the film begins, the performers are grouped in Warhol's studio as are the figures in Courbet's painting of 1855, L'Atelier... There is no simple order to the arrangement: people are seated on a couch, on hard-backed wooden chairs, and on stools; they are standing against a wall in the background. The whole scene is lit with a garish melodrama created not only by stationary lights, but also by portable Sun-Guns carried about by T-shirted technicians who wander into the frame occasionally to light a certain spot or move a microphone... The format is that of a variety show. People are introduced and they perform and act for a set period of time.

Paul Swan in an abbreviated gladiator costume which seems to be a series of oversized diapers does a death scene to the accompaniment of Wagner. He is asked to repeat it and does so. Baby Jane Holzer, wearing a poor boy sweater and wide-wale corduroy trousers, comes forward and dances with him, then disappears...

Mario Montez appears as a female impersonator dressed demurely in a long flowery dress. He sings *If I Could Shimmy Like My Sister Kate* and dances. As he dances, the cameraman zooms in and out. Never has the zoom been so gratuitously abused...

Mar-Mar, a chubby middle-aged man, dresses as a clown and deports himself as one. He wears two ties; a bow tie and a straight long tie. A teddy bear hangs on a chain from his belt like a codpiece. He delivers a parodistic political oration for William Buckley and performs a series of yo-yo tricks...

Jody Babb has been sitting on a stool swinging her leg in studied nervousness. Now the microphone is brought over to her. She announces she is going to sing a song although she only knows part of it. She detaches the microphone from its stand and walks around singing *Let Me Entertain You* in a halting, untrained voice...

At the opening of the second reel—some time has passed, but the camera has not moved—the M.C., Gerard Malanga, introduces himself and reads a poem entitled *Camp*, a short parody of Allen Ginsberg's *Howl*. It ends with the line, "Who would ever guess I was a boy?" Tally Brown, a very fat woman in a low-cut dress, just talks. None of us are really camping, she says, we're all playing ourselves, an observation as true as it is tautological.

Jack Smith refuses to perform... [17]

[17] Thom Andersen, "Film," *Artforum* (JUNE 1966), P.58.

INDEED, SMITH, NATTILY dressed in a suit, has so far shown remarkable restraint—even refusing to clap for the other performers, although he smirks as Tally Brown advances to the microphone. Introduced by her as "the inimitable Jack Smith," he makes a delayed entrance and, as the viewer wonders what it is he might do, stalls for time by placing a doll's head on the microphone and dancing to a bit of Ramsey Lewis's instrumental version *The In Crowd*, which has been playing somewhere off camera since the beginning of the second reel. [18]

IT SOON BECOMES APPARENT that Smith is going to break the established format by going to what might be termed the filmic interpersonal. "Should I open the closet," he asks the silent presence behind the camera, in an uninflected whine.

The question is repeated twice. Having donned shades and declared "let's open the closet now," Smith shuffles to another location in the Factory, the camera following him. Thus, the performer effectively commandeers the movie which, as Andersen notes, now

becomes increasingly incoherent. The portable lights and the microphone follow [Smith] only intermittently. Indistinctly, we hear the other performers getting up, moving around. Elsewhere are other voices saying words we can't discern... Smith passes by another couch on which two girls are sitting; when the camera passes, one gets up and walks way; the other remains seated, lit in silhouette. Finally the closet [a glass case containing a single Batman *comic book] is reached.* [19]

[18] Before introducing Smith, Brown makes a reference to her last "Warhol special," namely *Batman*.

[19] Andersen, OP.CIT.

SHOWN NOW IN CLOSE-UP clutching the key, Smith leers, feigns confusion, and rolls his eyes—posing, prancing to the music, and otherwise miming controlled hysteria. Ultimately, he is directing the action: "Bring the camera forward—is there a zoom on that?" Finally he hunkers down with a movie magazine as the next performer, FuFu Smith, begins to set up an arrangement of toy trains.

SMITH MADE HIS FINAL, BRIEF appearance for Warhol as a "soothsayer" in *Hedy*, shot in November 1965 from a script by Ronald Tavel. The large cast not only included former Smith superstar Mario Montez in the title role but also *Flaming Creature*'s Arnold Rockwood.

Marion and Frankie putting on
lipstick.
Marion dances (In black goosie)
(music started w/ dance + Bowles
tapes — goes on for rest of
film)
They form still fotografy
plastiques (with other people)

SILENCE Joana Vischer shot from high —
with lantern (stays w/
water bug — holds wears
white e.g.

Joana's
face → Frankie comes on to Marion.
a chase sequence.
earthquake starts they
look up at lantern swinging
Shot upside down (no
people — same camera set-up
that Joana was in)
They struggle (glass-shot)
SILENCE Last shot, Frankie's
pinned down under lantern
Marion faints — Joana rushes
in catches her and rushes off

Joana trucking — Marion
carried behind her.

The Snowstorm of Almond Petal
Moldiness Flaking.

Smirching Sequence.

1. Marion & Francine apply lipstick
(long sequence) (close ups of toothless
mouth w beard smirching makeup
on) (hags appear and disappear
in their costumes) (set gets cluttered)
(Naked men smirching lips) storm of
smirched tissues descends on
bodies smirching with legs in air.
an ass flexes to smirch lipstick
and sucks in the lipstick.
(sound track builds up with screams)(Slap the ass until lipstick falls
out)(a schoolmarm does slapping)

2. Marion & Francine pose about envying eachothers lips. ~~Marion dances~~
they drape about in front of backdrop & form stills. F.F. eyes (EQ starts
become inflamed. F.F. grabs at
M. the chase Marion strikes out with
purse. the clinch. F.F. pulls out
her tit. (E. ♥ builds up) (I record
myself issueing dialogue) (their answers
etc as take place if it were a silent
movie but with everything said)
C. U. of F.F. bouncing M's tit. Marion
screaming & struggling. ~~FF~~ Final shot
of many people holding M down as
F. slobbles her tit. F's erection
under his dress.

3

SILENCE

A coffin on the set – Veronica Jacks comes
out – petals on lid disappear. She sucks
Frankie Dry & they get up & two
step together which turns into
a production number. Sheila
and Judith return and kiss
Frankie (like a reunion) and
join prod no, including winos,
"Get right with God" & etc.

3. High L.S. chandalier. Mary

Posing about. Long sequence —
She has a lotus blossom. (in
teeth etc.)

4. C. Shot of bush petals falling
from it.

~~[struck out]~~

5. Mary showered with lotus
petals. (C. Shot.) (Very C.S.)

6. Ending in violent shaking)

6. High long shot. Petals come down.
F.F. under chandalier.
Marion stands stunned.
She puts her hand to her head.
and starts to swoon (her
bróp is still out.) Mary
rushes in & catches her &
carrys her off in her arms.
(Bells start clanging.)

7. M.S. Mary carrys her to
camera kissing her.

8. C. S. Marion reclining Mary
bending over her, their eyes
streaked with tears, they smile
and gage at eachother's eyes!
blossoms descend.
(violin music)

9. Mary puts Marion on a camel
and they ride off across the
desert — Mary's burnoose flowing.
(chorus of religious music swells)

J. HOBERMAN IS THE SENIOR FILM CRITIC for *The Village Voice* and a co-director of The Plaster Foundation. His books include *The Red Atlantis: Communist Culture in the Absence of Communism*, *Bridge of Light: Yiddish Fild Between Two Worlds*, and *Midnight Movies* (written with JONATHAN ROSENBAUM). In 1997 he curated the Jack Smith film retrospective at the American Museum of the Moving Image, which distributed much of the material in *On Flaming Creatures* as program notes.

BOOK DESIGN AND ILLUSTRATION BY
Chippy (Heung-Heung Chin)

TEXT AND COVER PRINTED ON
70 # Fortune Matte, 500 ppi
12 pt. C1S with matte lamination
AT
Thomson-Shore, Inc., Dexter, Michigan

FIRST EDITION: 1,500 COPIES
TEXT SET IN
Griffo Classico,
Legacy,
Mrs. Eaves Fractions
Opsmarck, and
Poetica Supplements.